PRISON TO PARADISE

PETER NARODNY

DENVER, COLORADO

Dedicated to my wife Karin, and my three sons
Nicholas, Alexander, and Marcus, who will
carry the family heritage forward.

Kim,
I hope you like the story
and its potential!

Peter Newdon

Contents

PART 1: PRISON

CHAPTER 1

THE PRISONER STARED at the beads of moisture trickle slowly down the sides of the cold stone walls, oblivious of the rat nibbling on his toes. His face was gaunt and deathly white with bulging veins running down his sunken cheeks. His long, filthy hair lay matted over his shoulders and covered his piercing eyes, bloodshot from years of desolation. His thick beard hung lifelessly down to his chest, and he found comfort in sucking on the ends of it while he shivered in the darkness. He pulled the threadbare blanket tighter around his shoulders and listened to the raging storm outside. With each flash of lightening he saw the markings that stretched across the wall - lines in the stone to record the passing of days. They added up to four years, three months and five days since he had been deposited here in total isolation, deep in the filthy bowels of this Russian hellhole.

The year was 1901. Predvaritelnavo Zaklutchenia was the infamous Russian prison that housed those political prisoners that the regime wanted quickly silenced. It was the House of Confinement, that covert penitentiary outside St. Petersburg where criminals of the State were sent to languish, never to be heard from again. He had been dragged to the fourth floor and placed in cell number 410 to begin his slow and agonizing slide into oblivion.

The prisoner's crime had been giving speeches and distributing writings against Czar Nicolas II, advocating his

3 ▶

abdication. He had been a delegate at several conferences and a leader of the revolutionary party. His last article was entitled *Rise Up*, which urged the people to take a stance for political freedom, and encouraged a revolution against the Czar. The article appeared in the underground papers and was quickly disseminated throughout the State. It was the final insult that forced the regime to take action.

A small barred opening high above the floor of his cell was his only connection to the outside world, but it did little to light up its desolate interior. It was too high to look through unless he perched precariously on the stool balanced on his small wooden table and even then, he could only catch a glimpse of the changing sky and the tops of the distant trees below. The momentary view of the outside world only intensified his depression, and he finally abandoned the exercise, in an attempt to stop the gloom from encroaching further into his already faltering consciousness.

His world was a ten by twelve foot space with a rough, cold, stone floor. The walls were cracked and damp, with gray moss growing in the crevices. A small sink trickled rusty water from the broken faucet, and the small open toilet was stained orange with feces, which sat for days before it was flushed. The prisoner had grown immune to the stench and found a strange contentment in lulling himself into a state of self-hypnosis by the droning sound of dripping water and buzzing insects.

He spent hours sitting on his hard bed, staring at the blackened wooden door, braced in four places with flat strips of metal hinges. At the bottom was a small opening, locked from the outside, and twice a day a small bowl of watered-down soup and stale bread was passed through and left on the floor. After eating, the prisoner would carefully position the empty tray and bowl close to the opening and wait for the same hairy hand to reach in and remove it. If there was no tray within reach, the hand would withdraw, which meant no food or drink for the day. Never a word was uttered between prisoner and guard. Once, starving for human contact, he grabbed the arm, only to be pushed roughly backwards onto the floor and left without food and water for two days.

The prisoner turned towards the small lead pipe that carried water to the sink and toilet. He held his breath and listened intently. There was a soft tapping coming from the pipe and he got up and dragged the stool over and sat next to it. From his first year of confinement he had heard the tapping, and soon discovered that the pipe served as a conduit for more than water. It was the means of communicating with other prisoners. When a new inmate beat randomly on the pipe there was a "lesson" given which started with a simple formula of taps, representing individual letters. He was soon able to read words and messages and would listen to "conversations" between other prisoners. As he became better at conversing, he began to recognize the senders and learned that their crimes were similar to his own. The interaction was a way of clinging to some semblance of sanity while time passed and his body wasted away. Now, brushing his hair back, he pressed his ear against the cold pipe. The incoming message said that another prisoner had died during the night and that his body was being dragged from his cell, soon to be replaced by yet another political miscreant. The message ended with a faintly tapped "May his soul rest in peace." Then there was silence, and the prisoner retreated back into his own private world of despair.

It was now the dead of winter and the bitter cold was taking its toll on at least one inmate a week. This only added to the quiet desperation of the prisoner's frame of mind and he was forced to confront the realization that with each death, it was only a matter of time before he too would fail to tap on the pipe for daily roll call. Groping his way back to his cot, he tried to sit upright, but drooped against the wall as he faced another night. The surrounding darkness shrouded the whole prison like an icy sarcophagus while he waited for the light of morning – or the warm relief of death itself, whichever came first.

CHAPTER **2**

MARIA WAS PERSPIRING when she took a bow before the huge audience after her astonishing voice finished spilling out passionate songs of revolution. As they applauded wildly, she moved quickly behind the curtain to catch her breath. The crowd screamed for more, but before she could turn back towards the stage, she was grabbed roughly from behind, dragged outside and thrown into the back of a truck. She was charged with conspiracy against the State and transported to prison where she was pushed into a grisly cell. Wearing only her long white dress, she started shivering from cold and fear. She attempted to keep warm by singing to herself, quietly at first, and then her voice swelled, filling the prison with a vibrancy never heard before within its walls. Instead of silencing her, the jailing warden sat in rapt attention, mesmerized by her songs, and overcome by the sheer purity of her voice. As the last notes faded in her throat, he turned towards a storage cupboard and reached for a thick, ragged blanket. Without a word, he passed it through the bars to her as a silent token of appreciation.

In the days that followed, the warden arranged for her to be moved to a warmer cell. In an unspoken agreement, she could expect extra food and blankets in exchange for singing to him daily. One day she sang an old Finnish folk song, which was one of the warden's favorites. It was a song of freedom, a song of dreams. He listened intently and told her that he had not heard that song since he was a little boy, and as a way of thanking her, he consented to smuggle out a letter.

The letter was a plea for help to Jaan Sibul, the President of the Russian Liberty Organization, a man whom she had met at one of her performances. After hearing her sing, he had approached her to express his admiration and the message of her songs. Now he received her letter and contacted an army general -- one of his covert followers -- and requested that the general make a call to the prison. When he reached the warden, insisting that her arrest had been a mistake and that she was to be released immediately, the warden agreed to free his caged songbird.

As he led her past the cells that housed the other prisoners, they held out their thin arms through the bars and waved goodbye, thanking her for the joy that she had brought them. She shuffled past the rows of cells, reaching out to touch their outstretched fingers. She could hear the silent sobbing behind her as she walked through the last door and into the chilling night.

Once outside, the warden took her hand and said, "Thank you, and may the grace of God go with you."

Nodding in acknowledgement, she watched as he turned and shuffled back, closing the metal door behind him quickly. She stood motionless, with mounds of deep snow all around her, not sure of her next step. Squinting in the dim light, she noticed a shadowed figure in the distance, sitting on a horse-drawn sleigh under a barren tree. She walked towards it, feeling the chill of snow falling into her thin boots, and approached the man sitting with a whip in his hand. Dressed in a long dark coat, top hat and scarf, he watched her as she cautiously came up to his side and without hesitation he said, "Quick! Get in!"

She recognized the voice immediately as that of Jaan, the man to whom she had written, and quickly climbed in behind him. He reached back and handed her a fur coat and warm boots, which she promptly put on.

"Get comfortable. We have a long journey ahead of us," he said.

"Where are we going?" she asked, incredulously.

"To Viborg in Finland."

"My God! Can you do that?"

"It's all arranged," he said, and with a crack of his whip they set off.

Travelling for hours through the night on narrow roads, their journey was marked only by the muffled sounds of hoofs in the snow, and the whistling of the wind as it swept around her chilling body. Flooded with emotions, she kept staring at the back of her rescuer until the first light of the new day appeared on the horizon.

Four men met them in the village outside a small cottage, and Jaan quickly jumped down and helped Maria off. Her face appeared frozen and starkly pale as she stood shivering in front of him. She reached out and took his gloved hands in hers, and her blue eyes shone in the early morning light.

"How can I ever thank you?" she said. They stared momentarily at each other. "Where are you going now?"

"I must get back. No one knows of my whereabouts and they must never know," he replied.

"You must be exhausted. Can't you stay and rest?"

"No, I must get back. They will give me food for the return trip. I will be all right. You are in good hands here. These are friends and they will take care of you."

"Will I see you again?"

"If it is meant to be, we will meet again. You must stay

here in Finland. Keep singing. You have a special gift, and good luck to you," he said.

Maria watched as he turned and got back into the sleigh that had been quickly outfitted with a fresh horse. She raised her hand to wave as his whip cracked and the horse reared, and he moved down the road, followed by clouds of snow.

It was her voice that won her freedom and it was her voice that now provided her with a livelihood. Travelling between the small Finnish towns and performing in concert halls and home gatherings, she quickly became popular.

She kept re-living the episode of her rescue and was increasingly desperate for any news of her savior. When she came across an underground newspaper that spoke of his work as a revolutionary, she cut out the accompanying photograph and pasted it on the wall next to her bed. As she drifted off to sleep at night, she prayed that she would see him again, and as time passed, her vision of reuniting became more vivid. When news arrived that Jaan had been arrested and executed, she mourned for weeks. When new reports filtered back that there was no verification of his execution, she quickly picked up her discarded dream.

Several years passed and Finland became a popular destination for Russian refugees, which put tremendous pressure on the Finnish government to return all refugees to Russia. Now as she sat and pondered her past, Maria realized that her future was tenuous, and she became very afraid.

CHAPTER **3**

DAYS DISSOLVED INTO weeks and Jaan lay in his cell without any awareness of the passage of time. His physical endurance in ruins, his life was sustained solely by his mental capacity for hope, and a desperate thread of faith that his mind wove into patterns of survival. In his dreams he was a traveler, journeying to a foreign country and living a role of leadership. It was a fantasy in which his mission of freedom for his people was gloriously fulfilled. Occasionally, he'd allow these visions to infect his waking moments, and a glimmer of a crusted smile would cross his lips as he imagined his new life. It was a life of liberty in a vibrant city, full of empathetic people with whom he could speak about the struggle of his people in Russia. Most of his days were passed in this delusionary state as he constructed images of this world that he might some day inhabit. This practice was the only element holding his fragile existence in place, but these hallucinations would most often be overrun by despair, and he would bang his head against the wall to remind himself of the reality of his situation.

His mind struggled with thoughts of his past life as a free man. He had fond memories of Maria, the beautiful revolutionary singer he had rescued from prison five years earlier, but those faded into the prevailing memories of his ruptured family, which were the most haunting. Not knowing the truth but fearing the worst, his feelings of guilt and sorrow mired him in abject depression. Now, even in his darkest moments, he could never let go of the belief that he would one day stand in the warm, clear light of freedom.

The violence of the storm raged through the night, and the prisoner lay on his cot with arms clasped tightly across his chest, staring into the darkness. He felt the claws moving up his leg and onto his lap and he reached out and covered the rat with his cold and trembling hands.

"Tsakki, my small friend, how goes the evening with you?" he whispered. The small beady eyes looked up at him and he broke off a tiny crumb of moldy bread and held it out. Nibbling eagerly, the rat settled into the curve of his lap, its wispy tail curling around its body in contentment. The absence of any interaction with something alive was devastating for the prisoner and his desire to speak was a mania for survival. He wished to communicate with everything: the clouds, the stars, the moon, and even his own hallucination, and so the prisoner and the adopted Tsakki would talk for hours.

"Tsakki, how old are you?"

The rat would close her eyes and the prisoner would hear, "I don't remember, for we don't measure time as you do. It is enough that we live and are happy."

"Do you have a family?" the prisoner asked.

Wagging her tail, she seemed to reply," I have my nest, my children and my friends. We live, love and are happy. Isn't that enough?"

She understood the speech of his eyes and he of hers. Once Tsakki's eyes were sad, like those of a weeping child.

"Tsakki, what is the matter?" he asked. "Have you lost one of your little ones? Has your beloved forsaken you?"

"Yes," she seemed to reply, "but I shall learn to forget and soon be happy again."

Tsakki was fond of music. The prisoner would hum a

tune and play on strands of his hair held taunt between his fingers and his teeth. Now Tsakki stayed curled up on his lap, frightened by the storm. Clutching each other, the prisoner and the rat trembled together and listened to the violence of the world outside.

A strange rustling sound coming from his cell window above shook the prisoner out of his stupor. He looked up but could see nothing in the darkness and waited for more lightening, which only cast the markings on the wall. He heard the sound again, as if something had been blown up against the bars and caught there, a branch perhaps, he thought, and the howling wind was causing the alien sound. He would wait for the morning light to investigate. He drifted off into his usual comatose state, interrupted frequently by his shivering and hacking cough, and the intermittent booming of thunder that shook the stagnant world around him.

The harbinger of the damp morning was the gentle tapping on the pipes. Another inmate died during the night and part of the roof had blown off, leaving several cells open to the elements. The news of the storm jolted the prisoner into remembering the noise he had heard in the window during the night. He left his morning conversation and stood on his cot and stared at the opening above him. He listened intently, and above the dripping aftermath of rain, he heard a distinct fluttering.

"That is no branch," he thought. With fervent curiosity, he pushed the small table against the wall and placed the stool on top of it. Using every ounce of strength, he clutched the slimy wall and inched his body upwards. His bare chest slid up against it until he could peer outside on to the ledge. There was something there, a bird, obviously caught in the storm and blown up against the side of the prison, and it had taken refuge in the small opening. With trembling hands, he reached out through the bars and gently cupped the bird in his hands, took it in, and held it close against his chest. It was shaking violently, frightened and injured, and yet it gave no resistance to the touch of a human hand. In agonizingly slow motion, the prisoner lowered himself back down to his bunk. With trembling excitement, he sat and gently dried it off with his thin blanket. He could feel the pounding of the small heart with his fingers as he watched its eyes droop, and then it slowly settled onto his lap. It was a dove with beautiful white and gray wings, one of which appeared injured and hung loosely at its side.

"Please don't die," he muttered to the bird. Tsakki crawled up next to him to investigate the intrusion and was quick to display her disapproval. With bristling fur, she approached the dying bird and the prisoner quickly picked her up and spoke gently into its ear. "It's okay Tsakki. He is hurt. Let us take care of him so he can get better and fly again."

The coaxing seemed to convince his jealous pet, and she reluctantly retreated to the floor. He tried to feed the bird leftover grains of rice but it just sat with eyes closed, and settled into the warmth of the human nest. The prisoner remained motionless and held it gently against his chest, rocking back and forth and begging for its life.

The feathered visitor seemed strangely comfortable in the man's presence and responded well to the gentle rubbing behind his neck, and its soft cooing gave the prisoner a fleeting moment of joy. He nurtured it with scraps of food and soon discovered that it had a small band wrapped around its right leg. He examined it closer and suddenly realized that this was no ordinary bird but someone's domestic pet -- a carrier dove! It must have been delivering a message when it was caught in the storm and blown up against the small window, and the message ripped off in the wind. Jaan sat in rapt silence as his mind raced, contemplating the implications of this discovery. His weakened heart pumped hard as his eyes bulged and he whispered a quiet, "Thank you."

The prisoner covered the window with a rag, which kept the cell dark but prevented the bird from escaping. Days passed and it would fly in circles and land on his outstretched hand, crawl up on to his shoulder, and coo softly in his ear. It was obviously content with its new home and yet anxious to fly again. Even Tsakki had grown to be accepting of his feathered friend and the three nurtured off each other - the rat with a new playmate and the wasted prisoner with a sprinkle of joy. "Whose dove is it?" He wondered. "Can I send a message back?" The thoughts consumed him as time passed and the bird recovered.

CHAPTER **4**

JAAN FIERCELY DEBATED his next move. He knew his motive to keep the bird in captivity was a selfish one since it obviously longed to take flight again, and he finally made the painful decision to set it free with a message attached. He realized that the discovery of his ploy would result in a quick execution, which would only bring an end to his decrepit existence.

The challenge of pen and ink was solved without much choice. He shaped a pen nib from a small piece of wire, and sharpened it against the wall. The paper came with his weekly lumps of wrapped sugar and now he had all the accouterments for a message -- except ink. His options were limited, and so in the pale damp light of his cell, like a skid row drug addict, he pricked the vein on his arm with his "pen" and drew drops of blood. Carefully dipping the point of his wire pen into his blood, he wrote one letter at a time. He struggled with the content of his message, limited by paper and ink and not knowing into whose hands the message might fall. Now in the gloomy shadow of his cell, he stooped over and wrote:

"Jaan Sibul, prisoner in Dom Predvaritelnavo Zaklutchenia. Please answer."

He regarded his handiwork and his arm which was now swollen and red. His excitement boiled over as he let the blood dry, then folded the message and carefully attached it with long strands of his hair to the bird's leg. Realizing it would soon be taking flight again, it trembled in anticipation and cooed softly, and like a fighter about to go into the ring, it walked in circles, bobbing up and down. Jaan picked it up, and in the crisp silence, he muttered, "Fly freely my friend. Thank you for the comfort you have brought me. Now go and kiss the sky. I will be here waiting."

He cupped the dove in his hand and carefully made his way up to the small window. He pulled away the cloth wrapped around the bars and with trembling hands, placed the excited bird on the ledge. The dove sat for a minute, blinked its beady eyes and turned for a last look at his friend. Then, with a quick shuffle to the edge, it jumped off, and Jaan hit his head on the bars as he tried to follow it down. He saw it come back into his line of vision and circle once, then twice, passing closer each time to his outstretched hands and then flew straight down to the distant forest below. He kept staring into the distance for a long time and then slowly lowered himself back down.

With sleepless anticipation, the prisoner anguished over his decision of setting the bird free with a message. He tried to convince himself that the dove's visit had been no accident, but rather some sort of divine response to his vision. Now his dream of freedom jumped back into existence, more vivid than ever, and like a faint voice in a cave, it pleaded with him not to give up.

His answer came in two weeks. It was dusk when the dove landed with a calm flurry on the ledge. Since its departure, Jaan had imagined the sound of its return so many times that now he didn't react, thinking it was just another mental rehearsal. The soft cooing shook him out of a restless stupor and he quickly made his way up to the window. Watching from below, Tsakki squeaked in excitement as

Jaan reached out and brought the bird into the cell and down to the floor.

It was still dark and the visibility poor, and when he felt the dove's leg, he realized there was a message attached. The other leg also appeared to have something on it -- a tiny pencil! With trembling fingers he detached the piece of paper and held it up to his eyes and strained to read the words, but the light was poor and he would have to wait until morning. He sat on his cot with his back against the wall, stroking the dove as it slept in his lap, fatigued from its flight and content to be back with his friend. Jaan's mind raced with excitement and as the early morning light seeped slowly through the window, he found his eyes focusing on the piece of paper. It was still too dark and his vision was poor, and he looked anxiously up at the window. Finally, he was able read the words:

"The dove brought me your message. She has a nest in my house and is my dearest friend. I know who you are and thought you had been executed. I cannot tell you who I am and no one can be trusted. Just know that there are many who believe in you. My dove is the best and he will keep us in communication. I send pencil and paper. God help you. Your friend, Miss Liberty"

He read the message over and over and tried to analyze the writing. It was neat and meticulous with a noticeable refinement in the penmanship. Jaan knew it had to be someone of the wealthy class since carrier doves were the mail service of the affluent and privileged few. The paper was of fine parchment with a separate piece for a reply. His mind raced for a profile of the sender. Miss Liberty could be the wife of an aristocrat, possibly even with the government, and she had obviously risked her life by replying to him. Interception by trained hawks was common since vital information was sold for large sums of money. The dove seemed pleased to be back in the cell and cooed at Tsakki who was excited about its return. It rested for two days while Jaan composed a response, asking for news of his family. He waited for the early morning and watched it disappear over the forest below.

The dove's arrival instilled a vigorous and renewed motivation in the prisoner. Like the embers of a fire stirred up by fresh wood, his mind sparked into renewed activity, and those dormant visions he had nurtured for so long, sprang back to life.

It returned in ten days. The message said that his estate had been destroyed and his family executed, but it was not known if some had escaped. This news intensified the unbearable guilt and brought more terrible suffering. As messages were exchanged over time, his suspicions about the sender became confirmed and the information she was sending could only have come from inside government sources, and yet the messages displayed support for his call for a revolution. He once asked for her name and the response came:

"You know the dove, you touch her feathers and pet her; I do the same. We both love her and she loves us. Is that not sufficient? She is the medium between you and me. Her eyes bring me your greetings and the story of your emotions and I ask her to bring you mine. I love her."

It was a dangerous game for the sender who appeared to have a passion for truth and justice, and a desire to end the suppression of the current regime. There was now even the implication of help reflected in messages like, *"All is not lost nor forgotten and know your fire can still burn for others."*

Although Jaan still believed the inevitable was nothing other than a slow death, his spark of freedom glowed brighter within his frail mind.

If indeed something could be done, his new friend did appear to have what it would take -- contacts and money -- and signing her notes as Miss Liberty had a special meaning.

As more time passed, the messages became sporadic and there was evidence that the dove had suffered a scrape with a hawk -- feathers missing and a damaged wing. Jaan knew the visits would end soon, and yet he refused to dwell on the implications of life without them.

Then the dove stopped coming. It had been a month since its last visit and Jaan sank back into a foreboding state of despair. Now his days were spent in a clouded, comatose state of consciousness while the fragile images of his feathered friend danced in his mind, becoming weaker with each passing day. If the dove had been captured, then the sender would be punished and orders would surely come to terminate him.

"*The dove seems to love its mission but grows weary with time.*" He read this last message over and over but there was no hint that it would be the last, yet he knew that a tired dove was an easy target for hawks.

Several more weeks passed and Jaan's psyche sank further. Lying inert on his cot, he painfully separated his crusted eyes and watched the dancing shadows of his tomb come into focus. He looked up to stare again at the light coming through the window above him. What had once been a glow at the end of a tunnel, an opening through which renewed sustenance of life had arrived, now faded and became a distant glimmer, and even painful to look at. His days were now spent listening intently for alien noises, for the sound of shuffling feathers or cooing, but only the tortuous dripping of the sink kept his attention, mesmerizing him into a deeper state of oblivion. Even in the midst of what appeared to be the end, he forced his faltering mind to keep a last ray of that dream he had so treasured. Something in the far reaches of his consciousness told him that God had not played a nasty trick on him for His own amusement.

CHAPTER **5**

THE PRISONER SAT in a lifeless heap in the corner of his cell. Two more tortuous weeks went by and Tsakki sat on his shoulder, entangled in his hair. It was past midnight and in the feverish chambers of his mind, he heard an unfamiliar sound - muffled steps and the clinking of keys. A tiny streak of light broke through the crack on the floor and he turned and stared at the door. He listened to a key turning and the grating sound of hinges. A large uniformed guard stood in front of him holding a lantern, filling the cell with a dim light. He took two steps towards the prisoner and stooped to see if there was any life in him, and Jaan stared blankly at the ghostly apparition before him. A giant of a man with a hard cold face, fiery eyes and bushy beard was looking down on him and he knew that his time had come. He was to be executed quickly in the middle of the night, and he felt a sense of relief.

"Come with me now." The voice came in a raspy whisper.

The crumpled figure stared up at the guard, unable to comprehend, then got on his hands and knees, looking for Tsakki. "My rat, I must find my rat," he said.

"Your *what?*" the guard asked incredulously. "No time, come now. *Quick!*" He reached down and grabbed Jaan under the arm and pulled him up. "Ahhhhh!" he stepped back and covered his nose, overcome by the stench. "Can you walk?" he asked.

"Yes, I think so." Jaan's voice was faint.

The guard walked back to the door and waited. Jaan hobbled over to him, and looked back at what had been his home for the last five years, and felt a sudden rush of sadness. Dazed, he turned to follow the guard down the long corridor. They came to a dark flight of stone steps and the guard supported him, burying his nose to escape the smell. At the next door, he waited for the prisoner limping behind him and panting from the exertion. There was a clanking of keys and the door opened, and a blast of cold air swept across Jaan's face, telling him he was now outside the prison. They walked faster and Jaan stumbled, falling to the ground, and the guard hoisted him back to his feet.

"You must move quickly," he whispered.

They walked further and Jaan looked around him, trying to make sense of his surroundings. The waning moon displayed a horse and wagon waiting on the cobblestone road, and a shrouded solitary driver sat with reins and whip in hand. The figure turned towards the guard and motioned to put the prisoner in the back of the wagon. He grabbed Jaan gruffly and shoved him onto the wooden floorboards, pulled a heavy canvas over him and told him to lie down.

The wagon lurched forward and his head banged against the sideboards. Dazed, he listened to the snort of the horse as it moved down the hill towards the forest below. Too stunned to comprehend what was happening to him, the rattled prisoner realized that this was no ordinary execution, and lay on the floorboards, bouncing to the rhythm of the fast trotting horse. He soon drifted into a semiconscious state with delirious visions of his pending destiny racing through his mind.

He lay covered for several hours before he became aware of a smoother ride in the wagon and a rhythmic clapping of the horse's hooves. He pushed himself up and peered outside.

Green trees flashed by in a blur and the cold air swept his long hair and beard to the sides of his face. He stared intently at the profile of the driver, trying to understand who it was that had stolen him and driven through the night. The figure had a small frame and wore a hood and cape, and stooped forward holding the reins.

The harbinger of dawn brought tiny bands of crimson streaking across the sky. Jaan heard the crack of a whip and a shout from the driver.

"*Hi Ya!*" It was a sharp crispy voice and the horse broke into a gallop.

"*My God! That voice!*" he thought, as the bouncing got more vigorous.

"*Hi Ya!*" The voice was louder now.

"That voice! "It's a woman's! It's Her! Miss Liberty!"

He sat bewildered by the possibility of what could be happening to him. His hands clutched the sides of the wagon as he stared out, mesmerized at the spectacle of lights from the distant homes. The emotional upheaval was overwhelming, and soon warm tears streaked across his face and disappeared into his tangled beard.

The horse slowed to a trot and Jaan raised the canvas again to peer outside. He could see the outskirts of a town while the sun cast a golden glow on the horizon. He looked up in the direction the horse was heading and in the distance saw a blue ribbon of water. The ocean! Again, his mind became drowned in turmoil.

They crossed narrow streets and passed rows of houses with clean, well-manicured yards. The horse was foaming at the mouth, its body glistening with sweat as it trotted on to a cobblestone street and down a hill towards the docks, the clip-clop of its hoofs echoing off the giant hulls of ships next to the dock. Jaan watched the spectacle unfold before him.

At the far end of the dock, the driver reared in the horse under the shadow of a large ship, steam pouring from its funnels and disappearing into the early morning sky. The horse tossed its head back and forth, impatient that it had to stand still so quickly after being forced to run all night. A thin bedraggled man was leaning against a lamp pole and stared intently at them from under his beret. The driver motioned to him, and he walked over quickly. The only other person visible was a large figure standing at the top of the gangplank with his hands in his pockets, smoking a pipe and watching from above. The thin man walked to the back of the wagon and motioned for Jaan to get off the wagon. He pushed himself up and stumbled to the ground before getting back on his feet. The driver turned to face him, moving the reins and whip into one hand and gestured to him to approach. He walked warily to the front of the horse and looked up into the half covered face of a woman with refined features, small eyes, and a firm mouth. With her elbows on her knees, she stared down at him, then picked up a small leather suitcase and brown package and gave them to him.

"Here," she said. "Take this. Now go! Quickly!" Their eyes locked together. "The captain expects you. Give him the package." She spoke in a strong, decisive Russian accent. "Good luck to you my friend."

With trembling hands, Jaan reached up and took the suitcase and package from her and gazed intently at her face. "How can I ever thank you?' His voice cracked.

"Just go. Live in freedom and don't forget your countrymen who believe in you. Please, say nothing about me. Now, hurry." She gave him a final nod, and with a slight crack of her whip, the horse snorted and pulled away.

Jaan watched her leave, then slowly limped towards the waiting ship. At the bottom of the gangplank steps he turned, but the wagon had already disappeared around the corner. He listened to the sound of the receding hooves and the creaking of the waiting ship. Followed closely by the thin man, he held tightly to the handrail and moved up the gangplank until he came face to face with the large bearded figure wearing a captain's hat whose cold steel eyes froze upon the pitiful looking creature that had just boarded his ship. Jaan passed him the package. They stared at each other and the captain took the pipe out of his mouth and spoke. "Go below. Follow that man. He will show you to your cabin. I will send you everything that you need. Take a bath. You smell. Have a good voyage."

Jaan tried to comprehend what he was being told. "Where is this ship going?"

"You are going to America."

"*My God!*" He stared at the captain in disbelief.

"We leave right away." He puffed on his pipe and motioned for him to move down the dim hallway.

CHAPTER **6**

JAAN VOMITED BACK his first meal, unable to cope with its richness. He gazed into the mirror and was shocked at his appearance. Over the next two days he cut his hair, trimmed his beard and bathed ten times, trying desperately to remove the stench from his body. He stared at his gaunt face and pasty skin, slapping himself periodically to insure that he wasn't dreaming. He walked over to the porthole and gazed at the surging ocean racing past him. He spent a long time just sitting and staring at the surroundings of his comfortable cabin, feeling the movement of the ship, and pondering the recent events in his life and what might be in store for him in America. He studied the contents of the small suitcase his liberator had given him. It contained some clothes and a roll of American money. His hands shook when he opened a brown leather folder to discover official papers granting him permission to live in America and assigning him a new identity. His name was now Ivan Narodny.

On the third day he felt strong enough to venture out of his cabin and on to the upper deck. He went to the railing and felt the sunshine on his face, relishing the sight of the open ocean. He breathed deeply, trying to clean out the years of collected mustiness from his lungs and savoring the freshness of the salt air. For the first time in years, he felt alive and his mind became flooded with all the same questions.

He was lost in thought when he looked to his side and noticed the captain standing alone, puffing on his pipe and staring at him. Ivan hesitated, and then with one hand sliding along the rail, he walked towards him and stood directly in front of stately figure.

The captain hesitated and looked around to see if anyone was watching before he spoke. "Are you okay?" His voice was strong and deep.

"Yes sir, I am. Can I ask you a question, Captain?"

"Yes, but I'm not sure I will be able to answer."

"How did I get here? You must know where I came from. Who was that woman who brought me here?"

The captain looked hard at him and took the pipe out of his mouth. "I cannot tell you her name but I can say that she holds a powerful position and she paid me handsomely to take you on board. She has done it for others as well and she took a big risk with you. Her only explanation was that you could do more good for Russia in America than you could by rotting in a cell. We knew each other from years ago and I owed her a favor. It took a long time planning and now you are a free man." He looked out to sea, then turned back to look at his passenger. "Now please go. I cannot be seen with you."

Ivan stared at him and nodded. "Thank you for what you have done."

The captain looked at him and his face softened for an instant as he gave a slight nod of acknowledgement, then turned and walked away.

The next day Ivan spent several hours staring out to the ocean and sucking in the clean air. He smelled his hands then spat in them, trying to remove the lingering odor. He closed his eyes and listened to the wind, trying desperately to rid himself of the memories of his damp grave.

He thought about how his dream for freedom had finally come true. "The power of thought is unbeknownst to man," he mused. "It was I that created this because I imagined the end result, and then providence took over." This mental exercise went on for some time before he opened his eyes and looked down at the passing ocean, and listened to the waves slapping against the ship's hull.

He stood motionless until he felt the presence of another person near him and turned towards the distant figure. It was a tall woman, wrapped in a scarf and long coat, and for a fleeting moment their eyes met. His cold stare and her soft gaze mingled in the stiff chilling breeze. Her golden hair cascaded from under her knitted hat and her beauty enthralled him. She stood erect, and walked slowly towards him.

"You are so pale and thin. Are you ill?" Her Russian was precise and her voice soft. She stared at him, and suddenly put her hand to her mouth and she sucked in her breath. In a whisper she said, "Wait! No, it can't be! Jaan! Is that you?" She bent forward for a better look at his face and took a step closer.

He was at a loss for words, confused and overwhelmed, as he focused on the figure in front of him. The woman watched him closely and her soft eyes sensed the struggle he was having. "Jaan, is it really you?"

He stared at her while his mind processed the reality of who this woman was.

"Maria? What are you doing on this ship?"

"I had to leave Finland. I have been there since you left me and they wanted to arrest me but I managed to escape. But you! I heard you had been executed!"

"They imprisoned me instead, to die a slower death. But tell me, how did you get on this ship?"

"I don't know exactly, except that it was all arranged by a committee for refugees, headed by a woman."

"That must be the same woman who rescued me!"

Ivan's eyes locked onto hers. The warm wind encircled their bodies and the world came to a standstill. Speechless, he turned towards the ocean, and stared intently at the horizon, trying to control the flood of emotions now breaking the surface. How could this be? Did his liberator realize that they had known each other in their fight for freedom or was it just a coincidence? He turned to Maria who was staring at him, her hair blowing against her cheeks.

"This is too much. I must go below," he said with hesitation.

"Yes, of course. Get some rest. You don't look well. This is a shock for both of us." She turned and walked slowly across the empty deck and through the far archway, her long hair flowing behind her.

Ivan stared after her, tightening his grip on the rail as he tried to grasp the meaning of the encounter. The serendipity of Maria being on the same ship taking them both to freedom was difficult to digest. He turned and walked back to his cabin where he languished in the trailing of her voice. He recalled that this was the same voice that had attracted him to her years ago as a singer, and the same person he himself had rescued from prison.

The next day he was back early at the rail, having spent a restless night of thought and anticipation. It wasn't until the early afternoon that she appeared suddenly at his side. He was lost in the movement of the ocean and startled by her presence.

"Are you feeling better Jaan?" she inquired. Her voice was

strong with the same lasting presence he remembered so well.

"Yes, thank you, much better," he said nervously.

"You look emaciated."

"I have been sick for a long time."

They stared at each other and the only sound came from the whistling wind and the slapping of the waves. A white seabird swooped down and gave a shrill screech before disappearing into the clouds. Ivan's gaze quickly shifted to the bird as he followed its journey into the sky, jarring memories of the dove.

She followed his stare and after a moment she spoke. "We are going to America! You and I together! You rescue me from prison and now we have both been given freedom. It is like a dream! Did you ever think that something like this could happen?"

There was another silence before he said, "Yes, Maria, in fact I did, but not like this." His voice got deeper. "In the beginning, I thought I was going to die. Others were dying every day all around me and I just waited my turn. Then one day I realized that I had a choice. I could wait in fear, or adopt a dream of survival. So I started to dream, and my dream turned into a belief." He took a breath. "It forced the thought of death out of my mind and I began having visions of freedom. The dream grew stronger, and the more I analyzed the impossibility of it all, the more resolute I became, and just when my body was about to give up, my dream was answered, brought to me on wings." He stared deeply into her eyes and quickly looked away, distracted by their intensity. She pushed some hair out of her eyes and moved closer to him, and his voice dropped. "I fostered that vision until it became the only part of my existence, and I never let go of it. There was an ocean in my dream! I saw tall buildings and heard everyone speaking English. It was so real that sometimes it frightened me. And now I wake up and am not sure if this is still part of the same vision or if in fact it is real."

She reached out and touched his shoulder. "Yes, Jaan, this is real. That vision is over and now you are living it."

He looked at her and said, "Maria, my name is no longer Jaan Sibul."

"What? Who are you?"

"Ivan. My name is now Ivan Narodny," he said, realizing it was the first time he had spoken the name.

"Narodny," she said. "That means people in the English language. You are of the people." She smiled at him as he pondered her words.

"Yes, I like that," he said. There was a silence before he spoke again. "Maria, as I realize what happened to me. I am overwhelmed by the incredible power of the mind, the force that one carries within them and of which most people are unaware. I now know that dreams can come true, and sometimes far better than ever expected, if you just hold on to them long enough with unwavering belief." He kept his eyes transfixed on hers. "I must confess that the only part I did not have in my dream was you Maria. I often thought of you and your singing, but I never dreamt that I would ever see you again."

She absorbed his words. "Jaan," she said. "I mean Ivan, I too had a dream. It was to see you again. After you rescued me from prison, I never stopped thinking of you, and when I heard that you had been executed, I did not want to believe it and was determined to keep my dream alive. When I sang, I thought of you, and somehow our dreams took root together, and now here we are, on the same ship moving towards the same freedom. Ivan, this force you speak of. It frightens me with its power."

He reached out and took her hand. She gently squeezed his thin fingers and held on to them. Together they turned and watched the sun disappear behind a cloud, and when he looked back at her, the fading sky had cast a glow on her cheeks and he found himself with more stifled emotions. "Your voice, Maria. It is as beautiful as I remember it. Have you been singing?"

"Yes, music has been my life. It is how I made a living."

"Will you sing and play in America?"

"It is part of my dream. To sing to the audiences of free America."

"It will be a great honor for America to hear you sing," he said.

"And you, what will you do?"

"I have a vision of a free Russia. It is a mission I have to fulfill."

They came closer together, holding hands and stared long into each other's eyes.

Over the next several days they spent every minute together. Maria learned of what he had endured and the epic tale of his ultimate escape.

"Ivan, what happened to your wife and family?"

"I do not know for sure but I believe that most of the family was executed. The Cossacks murdered them and destroyed my home." He looked down and became silent and Maria reached out and touched his arm. "The hardest part for me has been living with the grief, the guilt, and the shame. That suffering will be with me for the rest of my life."

They stared at each other and she reached out and put her arms around him, and he buried his face in her shoulder.

She held him close until the sobbing subsided, then he pulled away and walked slowly across the deck to his cabin, leaving her staring at his back.

CHAPTER **7**

IVAN AND MARIA shook with excitement as the ship steamed into New York harbor. They stood on the deck with tightness in their throats and mist in their eyes as they looked up at the Statue of Liberty coming slowly into view. Ivan blinked, trying to convince himself that it was real.

The complexity of their escape became apparent when two men in trench coats and hats approached them as they walked on to the dock. They were part of an intricate web of Russian refugees who offered an escort into town. Ivan inquired about the identity of the woman who had freed him and the men explained that she was the wife of a wealthy military officer who had secretly been liberating rebel Russians into various parts of the world for several years. She believed the Czar represented an evil empire and she sought freedom from his oppression by mounting worldwide support for a revolution, and she reached out to those with the influence that could support the cause. She had been a follower of Ivan and his writings and his avocation for the freedom from the "slavery of the people." When Ivan encouraged an armed revolution as being the only means of escape from the oppression, the woman recognized a crack in the impenetrable armor of the Czar. When he was imprisoned and reportedly executed, she felt betrayed and made plans to leave her husband and escape to Europe. Then Ivan's message from the dove changed everything, and she found herself with her own mission, on a path against the Czar and a way to disrupt the political mayhem of her country. She saw in Ivan a leader that could initiate a revolution from overseas and she used every influence she had to get him liberated to America.

Arrangements had been made for Ivan and Maria to live in a small apartment in Greenwich Village and within weeks they applied for citizenship and then quickly got married. The year was 1903 and news of his escape was never publicized while they searched for him in Russia and Finland. When it was finally discovered that he was living in America, the Czar offered 50,000 rubles for his capture or assassination. Despite the sizeable reward, his survival was critical to Russians in America and he became a "protected asset." When Ivan discovered the strength and size of the Russian underground dissident movement in New York, he felt safe. He also realized that despite the potential consequences, he could not be an effective leader by hiding.

His weapon had always been the pen, and now that he had the freedom of speech, he used it to become a prolific writer for publications in New York. His revolutionary theme against any oppressive society, and his call for help against the monster regime in Russia became quickly popular and attracted attention in all circles. His philosophy gave birth to several anti-establishment, anti-conformist movements in the United States and the birth of what was later labeled "The Beat Generation." The movement quickly spread throughout urban American youth and brought fame to Greenwich Village where Ivan had become a hero to that segment of American society. His popularity grew and he was celebrated as the most renowned Russian revolutionary in America. He soon held the influential position as leader of the "Russian Military Revolutionists," dedicated to raising funds for the armed overthrow of the oppressive Russian government. He was also appointed head of the Russian Chamber of Commerce which not only got the attention of the U.S. government, but of several notable writers and artists including Mark Twain and Robert Winthrop Chanler, about whom he later wrote a book, eulogizing his art.

When the Russian Consul announced in the *New York Times* that Ivan was operating under a fake name and had no affiliation with Russia, and that he posed a danger to America, he repudiated that he knew no other name and was acting on behalf of the Russians in America and the silent majority in Russia. Despite his exposure and growing prominence, there was never an attempt on his life and the reward for his capture became irrelevant as he immersed himself into his mission.

The crescendo of Ivan's work came when he found his dream aligned with that of some very influential leaders, and these affiliations with the elite were the most gratifying benefit of his role as a revolutionary. His friendship with Leon Tolstoy was no secret, and his last interview with him before Tolstoy died was publicized and brought many questions about Tolstoy himself. On April 11, 1906, Ivan hosted a dinner in New York for Mark Twain and Maxim Gorky as the principal spokesmen. Gorky had been a close friend of the late Chekhov and Tolstoy, and was a radical and a celebrated ex-prisoner of the Czar. The purpose of the dinner was to bring attention to the struggle of the Russian people and to raise money to aid the revolutionists. Twain himself was a self-avowed revolutionist and supporter of the freedom movement in Russia. He befriended Ivan and became one of his most avid supporters. Gorky had donated most of his own income to the movement and had been arrested frequently in Russia but was treated carefully because of his tremendous popularity. He was now in the United States to help Ivan and give support to a dream they both shared as vital to the survival of their country.

Gorky spoke to a packed center: "If we can build a Russian Republic to give to the persecuted people of the Czar's domain the same measure of freedom that we enjoy, let us go ahead and do it," he said. "I am most emphatically in sympathy with the movement now on foot in Russia to make the country free. I am certain it will be successful, as it deserves to be. Anybody, whose ancestors were in this country when we were trying to free ourselves from oppression, must sympathize with those who now are trying to do the same thing in Russia. The parallel I have just drawn only goes to show that it makes no difference whether the oppression is bitter or not; men with red, warm blood in their veins will not endure it, but will seek to cast it off. If we keep our hearts in this matter Russia will be free."

Gorky received thunderous applause as he gave his impassioned plea to the crammed hall. "I come to America expecting to find true and warm sympathizers among the American people for my suffering countrymen who are fighting so hard and bearing so bravely their martyrdom for freedom. Now is the time for revolution! Now is the time to overthrow the Czar! Now! Now! Now! But we need the sinews of war, the blood we will give ourselves. We need money, money, money! I come to you as a beggar that Russia may be free."

N.Y Times April 12, 1906

Ivan's efforts blossomed into what was a major thrust, which resulted in a series of revolutions in Russia in 1917, leading to overthrow of Czar Nicholas II, the last Russian Czar. Through the supply of capital and weapons raised by Ivan and his movement, the revolutionists were able to carry out their intent and throw Russia into turmoil. The situation got the attention of President Wilson who was persuaded to send troops to aid in the effort. He sent three regiments to Northern Russia and one division of 8,500 men that engaged in combat and defeated the Red Guard in a vicious battle.

Ivan learned of the successes and drawbacks in his country's revolution and realized that what was initiated as an uprising, took on a direction of its own and for that he was content to be in America, from where he might help bring positive changes to his homeland. He continued his passion for writing and published several books and articles. In *Echoes of Myself* he described episodes in his life, including his own imprisonment. He wrote of "The Golden Rules," describing a search for the subjective side of human life. "We must look to that which will combine knowledge, ethics and aesthetics into a harmonious whole." His goal was to "Help regulate a man's relationship to himself, to others and to mankind as a whole. May they lead to that infinite goal, which -- as the deepest truth, the highest beauty and the greatest freedom -- men call God."

Ivan Narodny

Mark Twain at the "A Club" house at a dinner for Maxim Gorky. Front row, L-R: Zinovy Peshkov (Gorky's adopted son and tranlator), Maxim Gorky, Mark Twain, and Ivan Narodny.

CHAPTER **8**

IVAN AND MARIA wallowed in the freedom of America, and the success of his role as a renowned Russian revolutionist brought him much acclaim. Maria also went on to achieve her own fame in music and opera. She performed in several opera houses and worked with Florenz Zeigfield who became her mentor and trusted benefactor. Her adjustment to America had not come easily, and the transition into a life of democracy and freedom was especially challenging. She was living the dream -- to sing and play her music without restriction, and as the reality of her freedom became realized, the result was a pouring forth of a passion and uncontained desire, which dazzled the American public. She became lost in her world of music, and would play the piano for hours, immersed in the memories of her past, relishing the satisfaction of being able to release all that lay inside her. It was her escape, and she expressed it without regret or anger, but with pure embellishment of what was possible from someone who came from so little.

Their only son Leo was born and named after his father's close relationship with Tolstoy. He was raised under the auspices of gifted and impassioned parents that often abandoned him while they travelled and performed. In the beginning, the young boy dreaded the loneliness, but as he matured, he became independent and read everything he could find; including encyclopedias and dictionaries which he took pleasure in memorizing. He learned to play the piano and was a brilliant student at Horace Mann School where he excelled in the sciences. From there he went on to Columbia University and got degrees in physics, optical and chemical engineering.

His father encouraged Leo to become an engineer and abandon his idea of pursuing a career in music, an innate passion inherited from his mother. Ivan believed his son would not be taking advantage of the opportunities that America offered, and Leo became introverted and despondent. He wanted desperately to fulfill his father's demands and with his gift of genius, he blossomed into a model student of the sciences. Upon his graduation from Columbia, Ivan lost his grip on Leo who quickly realized that the real money was not in science, but in the exciting stock market. He studied the dynamics of the market and discovered that he had the inner gift of "knowing" when stocks were going to move, especially with those companies that were on the cutting edge of scientific discoveries, and he went on to create a Wall Street firm with his partner Jim. It was an instant success and Leo soon became entrenched in the world of a New York tycoon.

Ivan's health deteriorated and he moved with Maria to the small town of Litchfield, Connecticut where he became reclusive. He struggled with emphysema, a condition he had inherited from prison. When Leo came to visit, he found his father reserved and struggling with his debilitating disease, and watching him, Leo felt helpless and full of regret. His father had never shared with him the saga of his life as a Russian revolutionary. He only knew what he had read in the papers, and for this he felt deprived. Only once as a boy did he overhear him speaking of his imprisonment to some close friends. It was a bitter cold night in Greenwich Village when Leo was twelve. There were three people in the small apartment - Mark

Twain, a Russian refugee, and his mother. Leo watched them from the shadows of the back room as Ivan spoke in the dim light, not aware that his son was listening and absorbing every word that came across the smoke-filled room. He heard him describe his prison ordeal and express his satisfaction in bringing justice to his country through his revolutionary efforts. Leo watched Mark Twain under the hazy light, puffing on his corncob pipe with legs crossed, enthralled by what Ivan was saying. It was an evening Leo never forgot and when Leo got up the courage to confess to his father that he had overheard the conversation and asked if he could tell him more, he was admonished and scolded for eavesdropping. He said his past was too painful and did not want to discuss it.

When Leo begged his mother to tell him what really happened to his father, she looked at him despondently and said softly, "Not now, my son. There is much to tell, but not now."

Sitting at their home in Litchfield years later, Leo watched his father get up slowly from his chair. "Are you going to bed Father?" Leo asked.

"Yes, son, I am. Good-bye, and thank you for coming to visit." He walked to his room and quietly closed the door behind him.

Leo turned and looked at his mother. They were sitting together on the soft couch and she reached out and took his hand in hers.

"Mother, it is time, I need to know more about him."

"Yes, you are right. It is time."

A light rain fell outside of their small cottage as he sat and listened to his mother speak in her gentle voice. He was mesmerized by the words being tossed at him and tried desperately to grasp their significance, knowing in his heart that this is what he had wanted to hear all his life. She spoke of Ivan's background, his first family, his writings and resulting incarceration. She related the saga of his escape, the execution of his first wife and children, and the insurmountable guilt he had carried with him, coupled with his lasting success as a leading revolutionary. With tears moving down her face, she talked about the satisfaction they had felt in escaping from Russia and finally living a life of freedom. She spoke of her being one of the first Russians to sing at some of the great opera houses, and the American friendships they had developed which helped render the support for the revolution. The tears kept coming as she spoke of the power of a dream, which is what carried them to freedom and provided the impetus for the revolution back home.

She looked into Leo's eyes and the catharsis left her drained. She wished for peace in her son's heart, having relieved the burden she had carried for so long but was forbidden to unload.

"My child, your father was a warrior who fought fierce battles with his mind. He loved you very much. He was just not equipped to show it. All I ask is that you respect who he was and what he did."

"I do, Mother. I just wish he had told me all this himself."

Her mouth twitched slightly. "In the beginning he suffered much from his persistent passion for writing -- which he knew resulted in the death of his wife and children and his own imprisonment. This was the sin for which he never forgave himself and tried so desperately to block out. Can you understand that?"

"Yes, Mother, I can."

"That is why he didn't like to talk about it. That night you heard him in the apartment in the city, he was around people who needed to know what it was like for him in Russia, and it was the first time I had heard him speak of it to others. I pleaded with him for years to talk to you because I knew what it was doing to both of you, but he couldn't bring himself to do that. He was afraid of re-living the pain and of you thinking less of him," she said.

"Why didn't he ever go back to Russia?"

"He would have been captured and executed. Besides, there was nothing left for him there except bitter memories."

"Did he know for certain that his wife and children were killed?"

"Not in the beginning. The lady with the dove told him that the Cossacks had come to his estate, murdered his family and burned everything to the ground. He still doesn't know if any survived. All the time he lay in his cell he had feared the worse but could only hope, and when he found out, the guilt almost crushed him."

There was a silence before Leo spoke again. "I just wish I knew all this growing up. It would have made such a difference." Leo stared at the raindrops that formed patterns on the windowpanes. "Mother, you talk so much about the pursuit of dreams. What choice did he have but to do what he did? It is almost as if his life was predestined."

"The only choice would have been to have given up his writings," she said. "He had been given many warnings which he ignored. He couldn't stop writing. It was in his blood, and he saw it as the only way to make a difference."

"What do you think he should have done?" Leo asked, swamped with emotion.

"There is no going backwards, no changing the past. One cannot live a life of regrets, for that will just suffocate you. We can only learn from them. For myself, I always idolized your father. He was a hero in his country at a time when there were very few heroes. I believe that if he had not done what he did, Russia would still be under the vice of a Czar. I believe that nothing happens by accident and that it was his calling, his dream, for which he sacrificed everything he had. I thank the day he stepped foot on that ship and praise the benefactor who saved us both. I also believe that it was no coincidence but part of a divine plan. If none of that had happened, you and I would not be here talking and the world would have been deprived of another great soul."

"Thank you for saying that, Mother. You always had a way of making me feel wanted." Leo's eyes blazed with pride. "Mother, how do you think it came to pass that you and father ended up together?"

She looked deeply into his moist eyes and said, "My son, this may be the greatest lesson that he has left you. It is the unlimited power of a vision. All that you believe shall come to pass if held in the heart with a passion. He did not envision the consequences. He just had to live the dream. My own vision of freedom carried me through my years as a refugee, and then our dreams came together as one. If you adopt any vision with enduring passion, it will be fulfilled. The power of the mind is astonishing, and it saddened him to see that most men are ignorant of that power, and do not take advantage of it. Do you understand that?"

"I do, Mother, and you have given me much to think about."

There was more silence. She looked at him and held out her hand. "Come closer to me."

Leo came over and put his arm around her. They looked long into each other's eyes and she could feel the fear and hurt in his heart. She reached over and gently stroked his face and the silence lasted for a long time. The white curtains fluttered silently in the breeze, as if a spirit had entered through the window.

"Will you forgive your father?"

"For what, Mother?"

"For not speaking of his past and for believing he knew what was best for you."

"Yes, Mother, I do."

Sitting on the leather seat on the train back to New York, Leo stared blankly out the dirty window as shadows of buildings flashed past him. The sentiments of guilt, fear and relief moved through him, and he pondered his new sense of responsibility and uncertainty. What has to happen to a man that he stops communicating with his loved ones? He pondered. He was afraid this could become his inheritance that he might bestow on to his own family. He felt that he had lost a great mentor in his father and an irreplaceable opportunity to reap from a lifetime of wisdom and insight. He stared blankly at the glass window and sporadic flashes of light lit up his face. Silhouettes streamed past him as he immersed himself in his own reflection. He was oblivious of the fresh warm tears pouring tiny ribbons down his cheeks as they raced against the droplets of rain on the outside of his window. The tears made slow circuitous route downwards, and dropped off his chin and onto his cold hands. He contemplated the new life that lay before him and shivered, pulling his sweater tighter around his neck.

CHAPTER **9**

"THIS MORNING THE body of a teenager was found hanging in the basement of an apartment building on 42nd Street." The television reported the murder as Leo stood by the window of his posh apartment and stared down at the street thirty floors below. His eyes followed the police car weaving through traffic, its flashing lights and blazing siren seemingly ignored as it made its way through the crowd. Now the news switched to the gathering momentum of the German army. He walked over and adjusted the rabbit ears for better reception but when the announcer turned to yet another murder in the city, he sighed, shut it off, and sat down at his piano.

The apartment was large by the city's standards with one bedroom, a living room, kitchen, and separate dining room, all decorated in traditional styles and colors, none of which really excited him. The piano sat in the corner, next to a tired looking palm fern that reached its dusty fronds towards the oil painting of his frowning father. Closing his eyes, he listened to the distant siren and let out a breath. He put his hands to the keys and waited. His shoulders sagged and his hands fell back into his lap. As it had happened so many times before, he had lost the incentive to play.

"Why do I feel so imprisoned?" he thought, and reached for the cocktail sitting on the piano as his mind drifted to images of his aging mother and father. He opened his eyes and glanced down at the keyboard and slowly lowered his hands onto the keys. His fingers responded, moving seemingly of their own volition, bringing forth a piece his mother had taught him when he was twelve. He played into the evening, lost in the ardor of the music until fatigue set in.

Lying in his small bed, he once again got lost in his repository of past memories. When the thoughts drifted back to the conversation with his mother, the remorse and grief returned over the sense of unfulfilled emptiness and unrequited love. He felt regret over the lack of intimacy and the distance he had been required to keep from his father. For reasons he did not understand until now, his father had chosen to lead the life of an introvert, despite his role as an avid revolutionary. Now Leo understood that his writings and imprisonment caused the loss of his first family, and his function as a revolutionary brought with it a fear for his life, but Leo felt sad that he had never shared that fear with him and never had the opportunity to treat his father like the hero that he was.

Leo loved his role as a stockbroker in a company he started with his partner Jim. The company grew and prospered, and yet he was developing a growing distaste for the lifestyle that came with the success. Despite the vibrancy of the city, he felt alone, always having to prove himself to people he didn't really know or care for, and he was beginning to visualize something different for himself. He longed for a simpler life in a more natural environment, an escape from the city to a place where the simplicity of life itself would allow a true sense of freedom. He never shared this vision with anyone because he doubted that such a place existed, but now he felt this desire for escape stronger than ever and a willingness to chase that dream that his mother spoke about.

His weekends were filled with a social bustle of meaningless and consumptive engagements in which he took very little interest, yet in which he felt obligated to participate. One of the harbingers of summer was college graduation, and Jim invited him to his sister's graduation from Vassar College. Leo accepted with rare enthusiasm since it was an opportunity to get out of the city and break away from the quagmire which seemed to be sucking him in deeper every day.

The Poughkeepsie campus was two hours north of Manhattan and it was a sunny day when they made their way out of the city. Leo was nursing a hangover while Jim drove past the stately buildings and breathtaking views along the Hudson River. The college was alive with the bustle of excited, giggling girls scurrying around; their flowing dresses displayed an array of colors as they made their way to the campus pageant. This was their graduation parade where the most talented and beautiful of the girls were paraded in all their resplendent beauty. Leo watched the spectacle intently; peering over bobbing heads while the princesses drove by, sitting nervously in the backs of the open convertibles, waving enthusiastically to the crowds that lined the street.

It happened in an instant. A quick glimpse and then a second glance that evolved into a fleeting moment of anchored eye contact. His heart surged. The beauty princess -- Mary Rogers, whose name was emblazoned on the side of the car -- left him breathless and staring long after it had passed.

Leo grabbed Jim by the arm. "Jim, that girl! Who was that?" His gaze was still locked on the moving car. He glanced at Jim who was watching him with a bemused look on his face.

"That's Mary, Cindy's roommate. Pretty isn't she?"

"Your sister, Cindy?"

"Yes, that Cindy. Mary is the daughter of a prominent family from Massachusetts; I think her father is the mayor of Braintree. Would you like to meet her?" Jim asked.

"Yes, I'd like that very much." Leo kept nodding.

"Jesus Leo, you look like you've seen a ghost."

"It's just that she had the most beautiful smile."

"Yeah, right Leo, and I'm sure you liked the color of her dress, too. Let's go find her, shall we?"

The two men followed the small procession to the reception hall. It was packed with crowds of happy faces echoing a cacophony of music and voices against the massive walls. Leo's eyes roamed back and forth until he walked into Jim's back.

"For Christ sake Leo, take it easy! There she is over there."

The girls were talking excitedly to a circle of friends when the two men approached. They stopped and looked up at them.

"Leo, this is my sister Cindy, and this is Mary. Leo and I work together," Jim said with a gleam in his eye.

"Pleased to meet you," the girls said in unison, holding out their hands.

Leo shook Cindy's hand, and then reached out for Mary's. As he looked into her face, he mumbled, "Never have I experienced such beauty."

Unaccustomed to such gushing emotion, Mary stared back at him. "Thank you. That is very nice of you."

"Well!" said Jim, interrupting the display, "shall we get ourselves some drinks?" They moved through the crowd, grabbed martinis off a passing tray, and drifted over to a place where they could talk. As their conversation progressed, Leo became more and more enamored with his find. Mary, in turn, was fascinated by this dashing stockbroker from New York, and flattered that he should give her such attention. As the band played a slow waltz, Leo asked her to dance. An inflexible dancer, he had difficulty keeping up with his partner who had obviously been trained in the social graces. He gazed fondly at his grand discovery with a sense of elation and freedom he'd never felt before. And she, equally smitten, got a deep sense of unique satisfaction and excitement from his nearness. She hoped that this was not be the last she would see of this man and by the end of the evening, she was sure it wasn't.

In the weeks that followed, Leo and Mary spent a small fortune on phone calls, jabbering excitedly about everything and nothing, recounting the events of their days and planning for the coming weekends when they could see each other again. Every Friday night she was on the train to New York, and Leo would take her into the heart of the city and expose her to the life he had been living, and she devoured every minute of it.

The budding romance forced Leo to spend less time with his parents, which left him with mixed feelings, few of which were guilt. Working with a lack of experience in the art of romance, he wanted desperately to create an impression on Mary and yet the biggest obstacle was her parents who took a dim view of her wanton behavior. Although impressed by Leo and his New York success, they were reluctant to release their grip on their precious daughter. Her father, William Rogers, was a ferocious disciplinarian and a powerful public figure who believed there could be no man truly worthy of his daughter.

Now that Mary's graduation was upon them, he realized that he was about to lose his control over her, and fought against the concept of this impending loss. On the other hand, Mary's mother Mabel was the true essence of a Massachusetts lady. Terrified of her dictatorial husband, Mable recognized the dire need for Mary to extricate herself from under his thumb. When the final nod of approval came, agreeing to her living on her own, Mary knew that it was her mother who had won the battle for her freedom, and was quickly numbed by the reality of the unknown world that awaited her.

CHAPTER **10**

JIM HAD DISCOVERED the great pleasure in traveling to relatively unknown corners of the world. He had been used to spending much of his free time with Leo, but Leo's preoccupation with Mary forced him to explore on his own, and his latest interest was visiting the islands of the Caribbean. He tried to persuade Leo to join him but he declined, now that his new love was so consuming of his time. He had no interest in leaving her to explore some "Primitive islands in the middle of nowhere".

When Jim arrived on the islands, he was content to play the role of tourist, but became intrigued by the descriptions of some of the lesser-known islands. Within a few days, he arranged passage on a small schooner going to the British island of Dominica, which was between the French islands of Martinique and Guadeloupe. Large by comparison to the rest of the West Indies, Dominica could only be reached by boat, and he got passage on a small trading schooner. After a rough, sea-tossed journey from Martinique, the boat lay anchored off the rugged coastline, and Jim waited to be taken ashore.

When he set foot on the island he was greeted by a horde of curious natives. The beauty of the island captivated him, and his short trek into the mountains revealed a verdant garden with lush rain forests, colorful waterfalls, and the ubiquitous sound of birds. Breathless from his discovery, Jim became infatuated by the island and his brief visit was enough to win his imagination and instill in him a determination to return.

He arrived back in New York bubbling with excitement and anxious to share it with Leo. He took the elevator to the twelfth floor, and nodding quickly to his secretary, he flung open the door to Leo's office and found him sitting by the window, staring absently out the window. He looked up at Jim with a distracted glance.

"Leo! You're not going to believe where I've been! I've got to tell you about my trip! It was…." He suddenly became aware of Leo's appearance with his tie hanging loosely around his neck, shirt wrinkled, and looking like he hadn't shaved in days. "Hey, what's wrong? You look terrible!"

Leo looked at him with a muddled expression. "What the hell are you talking about? Where did you go?" He reached for the cup of coffee sitting on his desk, took a slow sip, and stared at his partner.

"I found it Leo! I have found Paradise! The Garden of Eden! The most beautiful place in the world! It's an island called Dominica in the middle of the Caribbean. It's all mountains and rivers and jungle and I felt like a discoverer! The views were breathless and the people were so kind and…." Jim paused, realizing Leo was barely listening. "Hey, what the hell is wrong with you? You look like you haven't slept in days!"

"You'll have to tell me more about Dominica later. But while you were gone a lot has happened." Leo said.

Now concerned, Jim said, "What's going on?"

"Remember Mary, the girl from Vassar?"

"How could I forget, you've been glued to her ever since I introduced you." The phone on Leo's desk began to ring. Jim paused, expecting Leo to reach for it. "What about her?"

"Well, I am going to ask her to marry me but I don't want

her to live in New York. I'm going nuts here with this lifestyle. I was getting tired of it and now Mary has gotten a taste of it and likes it, and that frightens me. I don't want to subject her to it. She's too innocent." He took a breath, turning his gaze out the window, watching the pigeons land on the rooftop across the street.

"Jesus Christ Leo, I leave for a few weeks and you fall apart. I come back and you tell me you want to quit Wall Street, get married, and get out of town."

"I guess I went and fell in love with a woman and out of love with my life," Leo said.

Jim stared at his friend for a moment. "Well, I have just the cure. Dominica! Take a vacation and go visit. You'll come back a different person. In fact, I have a better idea. Let's buy some property there, build a home and take turns visiting it. I have to tell you. Your sanity will be restored, I promise."

Leo looked sharply at Jim and his eyes narrowed. "You're kidding. Dominica? I'm ready. I'll go visit and even stay a while. I need the break but I don't know about moving there permanently."

"Who said anything about living there permanently? If you don't like it, you can always come back, and it will cure what ails you, that's for sure. Now listen, I have information on a huge plot of land up in the mountains, two hundred acres owned by the government." His eyes were shining with excitement. "What do you say?"

Leo looked at his partner then put his hand out. "I have to be crazy but I have never seen you this excited before. If it's as beautiful as you say, then I'm in!"

In the weeks that followed, Leo shared the idea with Mary who had become totally enamored by New York and showed limited interest in Dominica, still trying to adapt to the changes that were taking place in her life. Meanwhile, the two stockbrokers moved quickly with their plans and purchased the land. Jim was to leave and start building a home but was suddenly taken ill and diagnosed with a rare form of bone cancer. Now forced to consider his choices more carefully, Leo got excited about the possibility of moving to the island on a permanent basis.

"Wait a minute Leo. You have never been to this island, and now you want to marry a girl who has never been further than New York, take her to live where there is nothing except forest, rivers and waterfalls. Are you nuts? You really think she'll even agree to that?"

"You don't know Mary. She just might. I've had it with New York. I've made enough to live on for a while and if she'll go, I'm out of here and you can come visit anytime. If this island doesn't work out, I'll find somewhere else to live." The adamancy of his expression made Jim realize the futility of any further discussion.

Leo's hope that Mary would warm to the idea of moving to the Caribbean proved to be wishful thinking. He proposed to her with the bombshell caveat that if she agreed to marry, they would not be settling in New York but moving to an isolated island, and the news came as a shock. The idea of marriage was exciting but the "travel plans" left some serious doubt in her mind. She had her heart set on New York and a "Swiss Family Robinson" lifestyle was not something she had envisioned for herself.

It was an agonizing decision for her. She spent much time alone hiking in the hills in Braintree, struggling with the concept of getting married and running off to a remote island with a man she had known for less than a year. She read as much as she could find about the island but the information was sparse. It sounded wild, mysterious, and exciting. When she discussed it with her brother Charles, he thought it was a "cool" idea but not one he would entertain himself. It was he who passed on the news to their parents before Mary had the chance.

Mary was in the backyard thinking about the marriage proposition and full of ambivalence. She walked up the back steps, opened the screen door and let it slam shut behind her. There was a momentary silence in the house and then she heard her father's booming voice coming from the living room.

"MARY! COME IN HERE! NOW!"

"Oh, my God!" she whispered to herself. "Charlie told them!"

Her parents were sitting next to each other on the overstuffed flowered couch. Her father's were arms folded tightly across his chest, his lips pressed taut, and his eyes were like beacons of fire. Her mother was twisting a small handkerchief into knots on her lap.

Mary stood in front of them with her hands clasped in front of her. "Yes, father?" Her voice was weak.

In a deceptively calm voice, he said, "Mary, is it true?" His eyes blazed up at her through his thick glasses.

There was momentary silence as she looked at both of them. "Yes, father, it is true. He asked me to marry him and I am considering it."

There was a dead silence before he spoke. "You will do no such thing! I refuse to let you marry him!"

Mary stared down at him, her eyes squinting. "You what? Refuse?" She glanced quickly at her mother. "Dad, this is not your decision. I am an adult now and I can make my own decisions."

His voice rose as his anger caught fire. "YOU WILL NOT MARRY THIS NUT CASE!" He lowered his voice. "He wants to go and live on an uncivilized island in some God-forsaken part of the world? You must be as mad as he is!" His clenched fist pounded the armrest of the sofa. "I will NOT allow my daughter to marry a demented dreamer who obviously has an irrational and preposterous idea of what life is all about. If he wants to escape to a deserted island, that's up to him, but he will not be taking you with him. I SAID NO!"

Mary stood with her eyes wide open and looked again at her mother pleadingly, but the only response she got was a slight shrug of her small shoulders.

"Dad, please! I love him!" She looked at him imploringly.

Now he was on his feet, standing directly in front of her. "*I SAID NO AND I MEAN NO! AND THAT IS FINAL!*"

Mary took a step back, then another. She looked down at the floor, turned, and walked towards the door. She paused, and slowly turned back. Her eyes narrowed as she spoke in a voice of icy calmness, directly at her father.

"You know what? I don't care if you approve. You have never seemed to approve of anything I do and I feel like I am in prison with you! Now you have just made my decision for me. I will marry him, with or without your consent. And if he wants to take me to a jungle to live, I will go, just to get away from this. I'm sorry, but I don't care what you think anymore. This is my life, not yours." She glared at them both, then turned and marched out of the room.

She reached the bottom of the staircase when she heard the shattering glass hit the wall behind her. Running quickly up the stairs and into her room, she closed and locked the door. She fell onto her bed and wept. Her pillow was damp with tears before she heard a gentle knock on the door.

"Mary, please let me in." Her mother's voice was shaking.

"Go away, Mother."

"I'm so sorry, Mary." She heard her mother walk away and quickly buried her head in her pillow.

CHAPTER **11**

"JUST TALK TO him. He'll come around." Leo pleaded with Mary to talk to her father who had turned virulent towards his daughter and the man who was taking her away. At the wedding ceremony her parents stood quietly, with her father having difficulty disguising his displeasure, and as the couple spoke their vows, he stood shaking his bowed head. Maria and Ivan stood across from them, their faces bursting with pride, despite Ivan's obvious physical condition.

They received an inordinate number of gifts which were a strange assortment of offerings, for no one really knew just what to give a couple about to embark on such an odd adventure. All the gifts, furniture, tools and household items, were put on a small ship chartered to pick up the cargo and delivered from New York to Dominica, a destination the captain had to research. Mary and Leo left New York and flew to Puerto Rico where they would catch a small plane to Martinique and then travel by boat to the island.

The year was 1942. The ship carrying their belongings embarked from New York on a sunny morning in early May and was travelling along the coast of Cuba when it was mistaken for a supply boat and torpedoed by a German submarine. It sank immediately with all six crewmembers on board. A tragic event and yet for the media, it was just another casualty of the expanding war effort.

Meanwhile, the Pan American "prop plane" taking the

newlyweds to the islands, ran into a severe storm off Puerto Rico and the shaken couple finally landed and took a small plane to Martinique with another bumpy landing on the small French island. Mary's face was deathly white and they were both drenched in sweat and rain when they checked into the small hotel. They learned that the boat taking them to Dominica was to depart the next day, and Mary was filled with trepidation after her plane ride, and quickly realized that she had never been on a boat before.

"I've changed my mind Leo, this was a terrible mistake. I just can't go on."

He looked at her in desperation. "We can't go back now. Let's push on and see how it is there. Please, let's go on."

"I just don't know. Right now, I am exhausted and all I want to do is sleep."

She collapsed into bed and the next day, after more pleading from Leo, reluctantly conceded to continue. They walked to the dock under a brilliant blue sky, carrying their stained leather suitcases. Mary looked nervously at the scene before her -- the motley looking crew, the filthy vessel bobbing up and down in the blazing sun, and the piercing eyes staring at her as she made her way gingerly across the short plank from the jetty to the moving deck. Wearing white shorts, her legs seemed to redden by the minute as she clutched the gunwales and looked back at the jetty and the growing crowd of natives. Feeling like specimens in a zoo, they stared back at the muttering crowd, and Mary grabbed on to a shroud when the slow rocking and uneasy sensation quickly overcame her. She pulled her hand away and glanced at the grease she had picked up and quickly wiped it off on her pants.

"Damn it! This is too much. I can't do this!" she said, looking imploringly at Leo.

"Let's go below to our cabin." Leo spoke quickly, realizing that she was about to get off the boat. She grimaced, and cautiously made her way down the steep ladder to the space below. It was stifling hot and stuffy and she held on tightly to the rungs of the ladder to control her trembling. She turned and looked around. The "cabin" consisted of a small box-like compartment just below the deck. She stepped gingerly onto a wooden crate to peer into what was no bigger than a closet, lit only by a small glass porthole that was shut tight. She quickly covered her mouth, nauseated by the putrid smell.

"My God, what the hell is this? I can't sleep in there!" She grabbed her suitcase and stumbled back up the ladder, only to stop short at the sight of the bustling crew coiling ropes on the deck as the boat pulled away from the dock.

"Damn it, Leo! We're leaving!" She looked frantically down at her husband, who stared blankly up at her.

There was a booming shout from the stern, and she turned to see the largest black man she had ever seen standing at the wheel. He was pointing to the sails and bellowing orders at his men. When he caught sight of her, he waved and said loudly, "Welcome aboard, Ma'am."

Mary stared in awe at the captain, realizing with a sinking feeling that she was not about to ask this giant to turn his boat around to take her back. She climbed gingerly down the first two rungs of the ladder before falling back into Leo's arms, knocking him back onto the floor.

Several moments passed before she stirred, her eyes focusing on Leo's sweating, anxious face. She pushed herself off and looked up at the patch of blue sky above her.

"Jesus, Leo, what happened? We're moving. The damn boat has left the dock! I want to get off!" She started to cry.

"Mary, you can't. Calm yourself, we'll be fine. You'll see."

She sat next to him on a wooden crate and buried her face in her hands. The sound of her sobbing was drowned out by the flapping sails and whistling wind.

More time passed and the boat began a slow undulating rocking. Mary was still sitting on a box labeled "Sugar Cane Rum," with her eyes closed. While Leo stared at his new bride, thinking that maybe it was all just part of an insane dream.

The calm sea, tropical breezes and the comforting beauty of the coast line ended abruptly when the boat hit the open ocean and began crossing the deep channel between the islands. Mary and Leo made their way back up to the deck for some fresh air while Mary's pale face was now tinged with green and she was soon hanging over the side, looking down into the rushing ocean as the boat rocked back and forth, crashing into every wave in its path. Her fading husband was soon beside her as they both vomited what little was left of their rushed breakfast of eggs and toast. When the nausea began to fade, Leo stood up and made his way back to the captain at the wheel. When he heard the offer of cash to turn the boat around, he just grinned.

"No mon, I can't do dat, if you want to go back, you have to swim!" His raucous laugh shook the pleading passenger who quickly made his way back to the side of his heaving wife.

They remained in the same position for an hour, until the captain laid a hand on Mary's shoulder and looked down on her with sea-scorched eyes. "Ma'am, you better drink dis and go down below. We be in Dominica in de morning." He held out a small tin cup with mint tea.

Mary stared at the cup before lifting it to her parched lips. She took a slow sip and looked up at the captain. "Thanks. Tomorrow?"

"Yes. Now drink it. You go feel better for sure."

She passed the cup to Leo and quickly turned to regurgitate the contents into the pitiless sea. Sweating and green, they slid down the companionway and stumbled onto the foul mattress where they lay comatose while their bodies adapted to the surging movement of the ocean.

Early the next morning the strong tropical wind had eased to a soft breeze and the boat had ceded to a gentle rocking that produced a slow creaking in the rigging. Sensing the difference, Mary opened her eyes and gently shook Leo who lay face up with his mouth open. Crawling out of her pit, she made her way above deck, leaving him groaning on the rancid mattress.

When she finally propped herself up against the gunwales and focused her eyes, she never expected the world that lay before her. The fresh warm breeze ruffled her tangled hair as she wiped her mouth, trying to clean the dry vomit from her face. The boat sliced the calm turquoise water, moving swiftly down the coast on the lee side of the island. Green mountains stretched up to the clouds and cascading waterfalls painted white ribbons down the face of rugged verdant cliffs. There was no sign of life on the passing shoreline except for an intermittent cluster of galvanized and thatched roofs and small canoes anchored off shore, bobbing up and down. She looked back at the captain, standing erect at the stern, his massive chest heaving under the shadow of the sail. His eyes were on her and he gestured towards the island.

"Dominica!" he said. "You have made it to paradise!"

She responded with a sheepish grin, and returned her gaze to the land before her. The water was a deep opaque blue, with small waves crashing against the rocky shore. In some places, the rugged terrain flattened out, becoming sloping miles of dense jungle. As the boat moved down the coast, isolated rainstorms cascaded against the green forests, and transparent white sheets disappeared as quickly as they'd started, only to form again someplace else. A kaleidoscope of rainbows danced languidly across the mountains, and through thin veils of rain she could see reflections of the rising sun. She was mesmerized by the breathtaking beauty, and felt her body slowly being restored to life.

When Leo finally joined her on the deck, his face was the color of flour.

"I thought I was going to die down there," he said, holding onto the rail to support his weak legs.

"Look, Leo!" she cried, ignoring his condition. "Just look at this island! It's the most beautiful thing I've ever seen!"

Leo followed her pointing finger. As the alien splendor passed before him, he too became transfixed. Weak and exhausted, they stood next to each other, and watched the unhurried storybook panorama unfurl itself before their eyes as a screeching frigate bird swooped down, announcing their arrival.

Mary on wedding day

PART 2: PARADISE

CHAPTER **12**

THE DUGOUT CANOES and hand-made rafts were full of naked children and half-clad men; their glistening bodies a striking sight against the turquoise ocean. The anchor splashed into the warm ocean and settled onto the sandy bottom off the main town of Roseau. There were no other vessels in the exposed harbor and Leo and Mary watched curiously as the small boats approached them. They converged below, bumping into the side of the schooner, as piercing eyes looked up in awe at the beautiful white woman and the handsome man. Mary waved and a boy laughed and waved back and they began speaking in a strange dialect.

"Garcon ! Gardey belle beke femme ca. Sou yoo ka fait ici?" A brown-skinned man said, looking up at the couple.

The captain was now at Mary's side. "Don't they speak English here? What are they saying?" she asked.

"They speak English but they prefer de Patois, the local French dialect. They say they never see a pretty white woman like you, ma'am, and they want to know why you come to their island." He chuckled then looked down at the natives.

"Tell them we came here to live."

"Tell them yourself, they want to hear you speak," the captain said.

Mary looked at the floating crowd below her. There was silence except for the lapping of water against the boat hulls and then she spoke loudly and clearly. "Thank you. My husband and I have come to live on your beautiful island. I hope we are welcome."

The brown-skinned man, holding on to the side of the boat, looked up at her with a wide grin. "Oui Bon Dieu! Yo ka reste ici!" He turned to the others in the boats and they began applauding and hitting the sides of their boats with conch shells as the small boys fell backwards into the water.

"Yeah mon, dat good. Welcome to Dominica," the man said loudly.

"You have any coins?" one small boy asked from the water, holding out an outstretched hand.

"Coins?" Mary looked quizzically at the captain next to her.

"Small change, Ma'am. Throw it in de water and they go dive for it," He said, smiling broadly.

Leo reached into his pocket and pulled out some loose coins and threw them into the ocean over the outstretched hands. Like a feeding frenzy of hungry sharks, the water became white with foam and bubbles as the sinewy bodies made their way below the surface, following the shimmering coins and scooping them up in their palms. Everyone was laughing and waving as a small open motor vessel made its way out to the boat to take them to the shore.

They pulled up to a dilapidated jetty and were greeted by a small crowd of curious locals. It was a sweltering hot day and Mary was still dressed in the same filthy shorts and Leo was sweating profusely in his khaki shirt and long pants. Their suitcases and boxes were passed up and dropped on the landing and Leo reached down to pick them up as a wave surged up between the wooden slats of the platform, covering their feet and soaking the luggage. Mary screamed and scurried up the ladder to the jetty while the giggling crowd let her get past.

Feeling dirty and uncomfortable, they followed the bare-foot man carrying their bags to the Paz Hotel, the only hotel in town. It was a short walk to the old, three story shingled building with large open doors into the bar and restaurant and a colorful veranda hanging over the sidewalk. The hotel was quaint and rustic, with no electricity or hot water. Coleman lamps sat on the small tables next to the bed, and the bathroom down the hall provided a slow, cool source of water, and after the accommodations on the boat, it was a small taste of luxury for the exhausted couple. They washed the grime and smell off their bodies by standing in the small concrete shower and scrubbing their bodies until their skin turned red. They devoured the warm meal of a delicious "callalou soup" and fresh fish, washed down with some local rum, then collapsed into the small beds and slept soundly, despite the buzzing of mosquitoes and the lingering sensation of the heaving boat.

Leo expected their boatload of supplies that had been pre-shipped, to be waiting for them when they arrived, but no one seemed to know anything about it. They wondered if the captain of the delivery boat either couldn't find the island, or had absconded with it all, and he sent a telegram to New York.

The next day they drove up to visit the land Leo had acquired, and he left Mary there to return to town to see if a response had come back about his missing shipment. When he returned, he found her sitting on a fallen tree, absorbed by the view of the mountains and valley below.

"Leo, I'm glad you're here. Look! This is where we will build our home. Look at this view!" She stopped short when she saw the look on his face and handed her the telegram. She took it and read:

SHIP W/ALL BELONGINGS SANK BY GERMAN TORPEDO OFF CUBA. ALL LOST ALONG W/CREW. SO SORRY. JIM.

Mary's hands trembled when she crumpled the message. Her hand went to her mouth and she looked imploringly at her speechless husband.

"Oh, my God! *This is terrible! All those people killed! And everything we own!"* Leo sat next to her and took her hand. She spoke slowly. "This is just great. Here we are, literally shipwrecked on this island in the middle of nowhere with nothing but a couple of beat-up suitcases. What in God's name are we going to do now?"

"We'll figure something out," he said. "Just think, we could have been on the same boat with all our stuff!"

She wasn't listening. "Those poor people. Killed because of us! I want to go back. Leo, all those gifts, and everything we were going to use for our home, everything! It's all gone! We can't stay here. I want to go back to the States." Tears poured out and her shoulders shook and she buried her face in her hands.

"Listen to me. It was all insured. I have some savings so we'll just get more stuff and start over." There was a long silence between them. Leo put his arm around her, waiting for her to stop crying.

She looked at him and spoke hauntingly. "Insured? You think they are going to pay us? Leo, that was an act of war! You think the insurance company is going to say oh sure, we'll send a check to an island no one has ever heard of for countless items we can't even prove were on a boat that was blown up by an enemy torpedo?"

Leo stared at her, absorbing her words. "We can at least try, and besides, we can't leave the island now because the hurricane season is almost upon us."

"Hurricanes? What are you talking about?"

"This time of year down here in the islands there is a danger of hurricanes and it is unsafe to travel."

"You never told me about any God damn hurricanes!" She shouted, and began sobbing uncontrollably. Leo tried to console her but she stood up and ran down a path and collapsed at the base of a tall Saman tree.

It was a long time before she sat up and wiped her swollen eyes against her sleeve. There was a rustling in the branches above her and a large chicken hawk spread its wings and flew off, screeching complaints about the intrusion. She looked up, gazing at its circular flight against the cloudless sky, and closed her eyes, listening to the bird songs and the whisper of the wind in the branches. She felt a light sprinkle of rainfall against her cheeks and slowly got to her feet and made her way back to the car, noticing how warm the rain felt. Leo was sitting at the wheel smoking a cigarette and without a word, started the engine and they followed the narrow road back to town.

The Paz Hotel was their home while they waited for the hurricane season to be over. It was now twilight after another meal of fish and vegetables, and Mary and Leo walked on to the veranda and looked out over the red rooftops at the Catholic Church in the distance. Its bells were clanging, reminding the faithful that it was time for evening worship. Mary listened and her attention was soon drawn to three women standing in the street below, laughing and gesturing with their hands. They carried baskets on their heads loaded with fruits and vegetables, and their voices sounded like cackling hens as they spoke Creole, touching one another and slapping their sides. When the group started moving away, one of the women looked up and waved.

"These people appear to have so little, and yet they are so happy," said Mary. "They're always laughing, always sharing, and don't seem to have a care in the world."

"Just like New York, isn't it?" Leo said with a giggle.

"Not exactly, but I like it," she said.

They turned to watch the street scene below and listened to the sounds -- a Creole conversation, a baby crying, laughter, a honking horn, a bicycle bell, a barking dog, and from high above, the shrill of birds heading out to the ocean.

CHAPTER **13**

"MY GOD, LEO, this is crazy!" Mary said, navigating the car through the narrow streets.

It was "Market Day" when farmers and shoppers descended on the town and cars and trucks inched their way along while the crowds crossed at random. Large wooden trays were set up along the streets to display an array of fresh fruits and vegetables, meat and fish, crab, crayfish, and items Mary was afraid to inquire about. No one seemed to be in a hurry, always stopping to gossip with gestures and laughter. It was a pace of everyday life that was drastically different from what they left behind in New York, and they relished it.

In the days that followed, they spent time discovering the outlying villages where the roads were narrow and sometimes crowded with pedestrians in no particular hurry. The island was a combination of rugged terrain, dense forests, and cascading waterfalls that flowed into the numerous rivers and out to the ocean and black sand beaches. The more they explored, the more enamoured they became by the beauty of the island and the frendliness of the people, and they felt at home.

Anxious to escape the incessant humidity of the town, they rented a home in the country on an estate called Springfield, owned by a wealthy American who had left the island. Built as a plantation home with many modern conveniences, the rooms opened up to a large veranda that commanded a view of the valley below from where they could hear the soothing sound of the river and feel the cool mountain breeze.

From their new home, it was a short drive up to the land. The 200-acre parcel was surrounded by rolling hills and a mountain range covered with dense vegetation, and a postcard view of the ocean in the distance. Mary held Leo's hand as they stared off into the distance, listening to the cacophony of birds and the gentle wind move through the thick virgin forest surrounding them.

"Leo, this has to be the most unbelievable view in the world. This is where we should build our house."

"What happened to returning to the U.S. as soon as hurricane season was over?"

"I'm having second thoughts. If we get an insurance settlement, I would like to at least try and build a home."

"If that's what you want to do, that's fine with me," he said, looking at her curiously.

"What shall we call it?"

"I've been thinking about that. Let's call it L'imprevu."

"What does that mean?"

"In French it means the unforeseen or the undiscovered, and the view, right?"

"The view in French is La vue," she said, "but I like the unforeseen, because that is certainly what happened to us."

"Then it should be L'imprevue, which means both, right?"

"Well, not exactly, but I like it. L'imprevue Estate. It sounds exotic."

He kissed her gently on the cheek. They sat on the grassy knoll and looked out over the valley and talked about living on the island and making a home for themselves and raising a family.

In a month they received word that the insurance company

would be paying for their loss, a decision which apparently only came after some prompting from Jim, Leo's partner. In the same mail, a letter arrived that Leo needed to return to New York because his father's condition had worsened.

"I must go, Mary. Do you want to come with me?"

There was little hesitation before she answered. "No, I will stay here and wait. You go back and see your parents and while you are there, get the funds and buy whatever we will need. I do not want to return. Not now."

He looked at her with surprise. "Very well, then. There's a boat leaving next week. I'll be back in a month. Are you going to be okay here by yourself?"

"Yes, I'll be fine. By the way, I know the kind of house I want to build. It's the design by Frank Lloyd Wright you had showed me. See if you can find some plans and we'll work with them, and while you're gone, I'll find a carpenter who can help us."

Leo thought he knew this shy woman from Vassar but he was beginning to understand that there was much more to her than he had realized. She was no longer the pretty college girl he married. She now wore a handkerchief tied around her head with no makeup; her white face began taking on a healthy tan, and her blue eyes shone with a spontaneous sparkle. Something about the island had awakened a dormant trait within her that concerned him, and he found her resolve somewhat threatening. He was also troubled by the possibility that once back in civilization, he would not want to return and take on this momentous project, and that would indeed be a test for their young marriage.

Now alone, Mary spent much time contemplating her situation. She felt that there was a reason she had come to the island, and intended to find out what it was. Time passed and she felt more liberated in the wild environment and its gentle people. It was an invigorating change from the structured, formal, pretentious life she had left behind in the States. The more frustrated she became with the oddities of the island, the more entranced she became by it all, and the more she learned about herself. The absence of the seemingly "essentials" of life like a pair of scissors, shampoo, or even hot water, which had initially caused tremendous anxiety, were no longer important. She was shown that eggs and lemon juice make the perfect shampoo, and an invigorating bath in the river left her cleaner than she had ever felt before.

A telegram from Leo said that his father had just died and he would have to stay longer, and Mary began to realize that he may not return, and she would have to make another vital decision. It was a relief when the last telegram came saying he was on his way back with most of what they would need to build their home.

He arrived two weeks later, looking pale and thin.

"How was New York?" she asked.

"It's crazier than ever and it was great seeing everyone again," he said excitedly. "They asked a lot questions and said how brave we were. 'I would love to do what you did,' they said, and then went on with their insane lifestyles without even thinking of doing anything different. I almost got dragged back into it and everyone thought I was nuts to return, and that I should just send for you. But here I am and it feels great!" Leo looked at her, suddenly realizing the change. "My God, look at you! You look marvelous! And I might add, very content. Are you?"

"Yes, Leo, I love it here. I feel like I belong here. Is that okay with you?"

"Of course, it is. That's why I'm back."

"So very sorry about your father. How is your mother doing?"

"She is coping but not easily. He died quietly and the funeral was small, which is what he would have wanted. I have someone who looks after her. Poor mother; she begged me not to leave her."

"So why did you?"

"What kind of question is that?"

"Leo, she's your mother. Her whole life is now you."

"What are you suggesting?"

"You could visit her while we build our home, and bring her down when we're finished."

He stared at her for a moment. "It's an idea, but not something I want to think about right now." He turned and slowly walked away.

CHAPTER 14

MARY LOOKED AT the check in her hands and clutched it to her heart. It was the insurance settlement for their loss and enough to stay on the island and build their dream home. The plans Leo brought back with him would capitalize on the breathtaking views of the surrounding mountain range, the valley below, and the cool invigorating breezes from the mountaintops. The long I-shaped home had four bedrooms, a large living room, kitchen, and veranda, and a long walkway open to the wild outdoors. The rich soil soon gave them a surplus of fresh fruit and vegetables, and with their chickens, cattle, and pigs, food was plentiful and life was good.

During the year it took to build the house, Leo researched the most productive use of the land and decided on citronella grass. This durable plant would grow freely, and the oil could be sold for the manufacture of soap, candles and mosquito repellent. With the war going on in Europe, the United States would purchase all that he could produce, and the profits looked promising. The stage was set and a large part of the land was cleared with access roads, laborers homes, and a "Still House" for the distillation of the grass into its valuable oil.

Citronella was similar to lemon grass, impervious to disease and animals, and the climate proved to be ideal. The natives cut the grass with machetes, then bundled and carried it to wagons pulled by a tractor that took it to the "Still House".

There it was ground up and sent into a giant vat for distillation, and cooked with intense heat coming from an enormous wood-burning boiler. The oil settled to the bottom where it was poured off and stored in giant bottles encased in wooden crates. These were transported and loaded on to a ship bound for the United States. It was a labor-intensive process and the time it took from cutting the grass to receiving a paycheck was several months.

Fascinated by the stories she was told by the locals, Mary studied the history of the island and the intriguing turmoil of its past. The earliest settlers were the Arawaks, an Indian tribe that travelled from South America and lived peacefully on the island for over a hundred years before they were invaded and conquered by the Caribs, a fierce and warlike tribe. Both cultures and languages became fused, and their simple lifestyle of fishing and growing crops continued for many years until Columbus discovered the island in 1492 on a Sunday, thus the name Dominica, from the Italian word for Sunday.

Visiting Europeans were continuously beaten back by the Caribs and it took many years before this ferocious tribe finally became accepting of the Europeans, and began trading their fresh fruit and produce for knives, glass, and tools.

The first French missionary landed in Dominica in 1642 and years later, the first Christian mass was celebrated on the island. The French had invaded several of the islands and took over the neighboring islands of Martinique and Guadeloupe but were no match for the Dominica Caribs who began raiding the nearby islands of Antigua, St. Lucia and St. Vincent. The French and English finally agreed to leave Dominica as a neutral island belonging to the Caribs. This lasted until 1727 when a French officer came to the island bringing its first slaves to assist in building plantations, and that population grew over the years to become the predominant race.

In 1761 England attacked Dominica with eight ships, and quickly declared it to be under English rule. 17 years later France launched a surprise attack on the island and the British surrendered, putting Dominica under the French flag. By this time, the population had swelled to over 16,000 of which 14,000 were slaves, and as the French influence grew, many of the settled colonists fled the island and returned to England. In 1779 another disastrous hurricane struck the island followed by a fire that leveled the main town of Roseau, leaving a disorganized and frustrated governor. More battles ensued between the British and French and the English were finally victorious and established Dominica as a colony of Britain.

The island's history depicted constant tribunals of hurricanes, attacks, food shortages and internal strife, and yet the plantation society survived with its slave labor. When slavery was abolished in 1835, the slaves were left to live on their own by occupying land and creating their own gardens. Life went on with the exodus of many of the landowners and white Colonists, and the island suffered from poverty and illiteracy. Those who stayed made their living from the fertile land, and exporting sugar, tobacco, and fresh crops to the surrounding islands.

The advent of World War I caused many of the remaining white families to leave the island and return home. In 1916 another devastating hurricane wiped out roads and bridges and the island's crops were destroyed. The recovery was a slow process and with the onset of World War II, the island's economy faltered once again, and yet the locals made the most of the rainfall and the richness of the soil and were able to live off the land.

The more Mary learned about the island, the more appreciation she had for the struggles the people had endured. She also realized there had been many white people -- British, French and Spanish -- that had settled on the island long before she got there but had returned to their homelands, and now only a few families remained scattered around the island. Various British settlers had made attempts to improve the island, which had fallen into a deep state of neglect as England became more and more unwilling to support it. Time passed and with limited funds, roads were constructed which improved the access to the remote villages and the production of cocoa, limes, sugar, coffee, coconuts and vanilla boosted the island's economy.

Mary's knowledge of the island's history made her more enamored by it all, and she wanted to make it her permanent home. Although the thought of raising children in the wild haunted her, she was euphoric when she got pregnant. As the pregnancy progressed, she questioned the island's facilities, and returned to New York to have the baby. After the birth of Penelope, she and Leo made a hasty retreat back to the island to live in their new home in the mountains.

Three years later Mary was again with child and this time she decided to remain on the island for the birth of Ivan, named after his grandfather, in the small hospital in Roseau. She was content with a boy and a girl and the news of another pregnancy caused much concern and dissension. Peter was born two years after Ivan and in the same bed, which was no coincidence since it was the only private room in the only hospital on the island.

Leo on his tractor

Penny, Ivan and Peter in truck on estate

CHAPTER 15

"THIS ISN'T WORKING Mary. I don't think I can go on." Leo sat on veranda and sipped on his third gin and tonic. He looked down at his glass and shook it, and the rattling ice filled the silence between them.

Mary sat quietly, watching him. "What exactly are you saying?"

"It's been ten years now, and this idea of living off the land and raising a family on this island. It's killing me."

"I see, and what do you intend to do about it?"

"I'm not sure, but right now I need another drink." He got up and walked into the living room. Mary heard the clink of the decanter, and then a door slam shut. She sat staring out at the rainbow forming over the mountain, and her mind raced.

Time passed and Leo's dream of distilling citronella grass and shipping the oil to the States was full of mounting challenges. The cost of the equipment, maintenance, and labor, had left them struggling financially. He now realized that not only did his concept require constant physical effort, but lacked any form of mental challenge, which for him and his brilliant mind, was belittling and boring. Discouraged and depressed, he saw his grand plan crumbling and looked for an escape.

He began traveling to the neighboring islands to seek other possibilities, leaving behind a befuddled and angry wife with two lost boys and a girl. Mary's frustration grew by having to care for them and cope with the problems of the estate, and she desperately sought solace and courage to endure the test that had been put before her.

Penny was sent to a boarding school in Barbados, and was only home for the holidays. Ivan and Peter, now six and four, found their lives revolve around their mother who had begun homeschooling them, but quickly realized that this was not a viable plan. The production of citronella ceased completely and the laborers replaced some of the fields with bananas. It was a crop that grew quickly and the island was exporting shiploads to England, but this idea did not come without its own struggles and setbacks, and proved to fall short of being any more profitable than citronella.

In her search for friendship and someone to converse with, Mary had been socializing with some of the locals and other white families on the island. At a cocktail party she met Hazel, an English woman and her artist husband, who had visited the island years before with the intent of capturing its incredible beauty on canvas. They had built a beautiful home overlooking the town, and it wasn't long before Mary and Hazel became close friends and with whom Mary could share her dilemma.

It was an early Saturday evening after Mary had put the boys to bed when she heard the truck pull into the garage, and heard his footsteps on the marble stairs. Leo walked into the kitchen, his hair hanging over his bloodshot eyes and his clothes were dripping wet. She kept washing the dishes, trying to ignore him.

"Well, are you going to at least say hello?" he said loudly, slurring his words.

She turned and wiped her hands on her apron. The only sound came from the kerosene Coleman lamp and the intermittent popping of the mantels. Her eyes got smaller and her voice was steady as she spoke with a slight tremor.

"Tell me," she said, "What do you want me to say? You have been gone for two weeks and no one knew where, the boys ask for you every day, and I have run out of stories about why you are never here. Peter was sick on his birthday and I had no car to take him to a doctor. I cannot take them to school and the estate is going to close down since the laborers have not been paid. You left me with no money to deal with all this and now you want me to welcome you home with open arms?"

He stared at her, holding on to the table to steady himself. "I'm sorry. I was visiting a friend." He looked down at the floor.

"I have had it with the drunkenness and the lies. Get the hell out of here!" She stormed past him, grabbing a pile of laundry off the back of the chair and slammed the door behind her. She heard him belch loudly as she walked away.

The next morning Mary came in and shook him out of his snoring slumber as he lay face up on the couch. "Get up before the boys find you here like this," she said. "Take a shower, and as far as I'm concerned, you can just go back to where you came from."

Leo muttered something and swung his feet on to the floor and watched her as she set the table for breakfast. He said nothing when he got up and made his way down the hall to the bathroom. The door flung open before him and both the boys came tumbling out.

"Daddy! Daddy!" They ran to him and he stooped to hug them.

"Where have you been?" They said in unison. They both leaned back and looked up, taken back by his appearance.

"I was on a business trip," he said.

"Did you bring me a present?" Peter asked.

"Sorry, but I was too busy, but next time."

"But, Daddy, it was my birthday last week," Peter said.

"Sorry, I forgot." He gazed at the boys for several moments then turned and walked away, leaving them staring at his back as he closed the door behind him. They quickly turned and ran up the steps to the road and disappeared into the bush.

Days went by and despondency hovered over the family. The relationship between Leo and Mary became more strained and the reality of their situation became painfully obvious.

Leo waited for an opportune time to talk to Mary. "What do you think of going back?"

"Going back where?" She squinted at him.

"To the States. There's nothing left for us here."

"For us, or for you?" Her eyes blazed as she stared at him. "I'm not going back Leo. You go. I'll find a way here. What am I going to do in New York, sit in an apartment while you figure out what to do with yourself? That place is more of a jungle than this is. Just go, and don't even think of taking the boys with you."

He looked at her glaring face. "Okay, pioneer woman, you stay here and keep the boys. I wouldn't know how to handle them in a civilized country anyway. They are like wild animals."

Her hands dropped. "My God, Leo, how dare you say that! They are your children! Why do you think they are wild? Maybe because they have no father! Have you ever thought of that?"

He was silent, then turned and walked away.

In the days that followed, the communication between them dwindled to trivial, unemotional statements while Leo planned his exit. Mary's suspicions were confirmed when she got a report from Hazel who said he was spotted in a restaurant in Barbados, having a warm conversation with the wife of a wealthy hotel owner. Mary was hurt and yet relieved, knowing that it was a confirmation of something she felt was inevitable.

It was a sultry afternoon and the boys had been hunting in the woods when they heard the old Ford truck pull up below the house and they ran to meet it. They watched from a short distance when the car door opened and Leo stumbled out. He was mumbling and disheveled as he groped for the handle, pulled himself onto his feet and brushed debris from his pants. The boys quickly retraced their steps and hid in the bushes and watched with wide eyes as he staggered up the road. He swore, and turned back to the Still House and his office, passing within a few feet of them. When he was out of sight, they looked at each other and ran quickly back to the house and into the small room where Mary was sewing. She looked up and saw the anguish on their faces.

"What happened?" she asked, putting down her sewing.

"It's Daddy! Something's wrong! He fell!" Ivan said, panting heavily.

She stretched out her arms and they ran to her. "Everything will be all right, not to worry. I'll find out what's wrong. Now run along to your room."

It was nightfall and the boys had the kerosene lamps turned down low, trying to read but were distracted by the commotion in the next room. They tiptoed to the door and listened. There was shouting and a crash, something thrown across the room and then silence. They heard their mother sobbing, more shouting, and another crash against the door. Terrified, they ran to the window, pushed it open and jumped to the ground, falling hard and rolling on to their sides. Peter groaned, grabbing his ankle, and limped after his brother who was running towards the woods. They sat hunched next each other in the darkness as a light rain fell, quickly soaking them in their pajamas, their stifled sobs absorbed by the thick vegetation surrounding them. They were unaware of the time that passed before they noticed the blackness around them.

"Can we go back now? I'm cold." Peter spoke slowly.

"Yes, let's go," Ivan whispered.

They moved stealthily, gazing at the silhouette of the house against the moonlit sky. Wet and exhausted, they climbed onto the veranda and into their room. Peeling off their clammy pajamas, they slipped naked under the cool sheets, and lay with eyes open, trying desperately to understand what was happening.

The next day they watched from a distance as Leo threw his suitcase into the back of the small truck and drove off, and this time, they didn't think he was coming back. The loss of their father caused much unrest, and they struggled to understand why, and quietly blamed themselves.

CHAPTER 16

THE LONLINESS OF the boy's lives was broken up by their own imagination, and they became friends with two dwarfs that lived in the base of a huge tree close to the house. This was an inspiration introduced when Peter discovered the natural opening of roots at the base of the large and ancient "Mammy Apple" tree. He got on his knees and peered inside, softly calling out, "Hey, Tonya! Hey, Baboo! Come out and play with me, will you?" The only response was the whistling wind while he sat and waited at its base. He leaned over again and whispered. "Okay, I'll bring you some food." He jumped up and raced back to the house, passing Ivan on the steps.

"Hey! Where you going?"

"To feed Tonya and Baboo," Peter responded, breathless.

"Who?"

"The two dwarfs that live in the tree! Quick! Come with me! They are hungry!"

They dashed into the kitchen and found some bread, stuffed it into their pockets and raced back. They placed the food next to the opening and waited for some time before Ivan spoke. "Where are these dwarfs you're talking about?"

"They don't like people to watch them when they eat," Peter answered, looking down at the bread.

"Okay, then let's leave them alone. This is so cool! What do they look like?" Ivan's excitement only encouraged his brother.

"Well, Tonya is the short one, about this tall, " he said,

holding his hand ten inches off the ground. "And Baboo is older and a little taller and fatter. They are furry with small eyes and pointed noses and very shy." He looked at Ivan with convincing eyes.

"I hope I get to see them."

"You will, but we have to go now so they can eat."

"Okay, let's go." They both scampered off with Ivan stopping momentarily to look back at the home of their new-found friends. They returned an hour later to find all the bread gone. Thrilled that the dwarfs had finally eaten, their excitement grew.

"Hey, they came out! They liked the bread," said Ivan as he looked down at Jumbie, their trusted dog, who was also looking at the tree and wagging his tail.

The relationship with the dwarfs grew as the boys played imaginary games, sang songs to them and left food at the opening in the "Dwarf Tree", much to the delight of Jumbie. Soon Tonya and Baboo were accompanying the boys on walks in the woods but kept their distance behind them. The boys would shuffle off together, shirtless and barefoot, giggling and talking as they walked through the bush, pointing at things and asking the dwarfs to hurry. As time passed however, Ivan's skepticism grew and he began to lose faith in the dwarf's existence, pointing out the possibility that it was in fact Jumbie that was eating the food they left at the tree. Nevertheless, Peter kept the dwarfs as companions, and they always seemed to be there when he needed a friend.

"We seem to spend a lot of time just waiting for something to happen." Ivan said, perched on a branch of the Mangosteen tree, picking the purple fruit, peeling back the outside skin and eating the white succulent insides that were soft and sweet. Peter sat on a branch across from him, their feet swinging beneath them thirty feet above the ground while Jumbie sat below them, waging her tail and catching everything that they dropped from above. They ate the fruit and gazed out through the branches at a rainbow forming in the distance. There was silence all around except for the wind and the ubiquitous birdsong.

Finally Peter spoke. "What do you mean?"

"Well, we wait for Daddy to come home. We wait for the weekend to go to town. We even wait for the night to go to sleep! We're always waiting for something to happen. Now I'm just waiting to be old enough to get out of here, to escape to someplace else!" He looked over at his brother and spat out more pulp and continued to swing his legs under him. "What are you waiting for?"

Peter kept chewing and looked at him, the white meat of the mangosteen smeared on his cheeks. "Right now I'm just waiting for you to shut up," he said.

Ivan looked sideways at him, then turned, and with perfect aim, spat a piece of white pulp that stuck to Peter's cheek. What would have been the beginning of another brawl was impaired by their precarious location. Instead, a pulp-spitting contest ensued which soon faltered as the supply diminished and their faces were covered with drooping pulp. They both laughed and picked their faces clean, throwing the last pieces of fruit into their mouths.

They sat for a moment in silence high above the ground before Peter broke the silence. "Hey, you know what tomorrow is?"

"Saturday, and I can hardly wait. Town time, and I am going to get the new Superman comic!"

They turned to peer through the branches and watch as the virulent sun sank behind the distant horizon. They could feel the heat of the day dissipating and like monkeys, they swung down from branch to branch, landing softly on the ground where Jumbie was waiting.

They were up early the next day and ran to the breakfast table when they heard the clanging of the bell. Mary was already seated when they walked in.

"Ready for town?" She asked.

"Oh, yeah!" they said in unison.

The meal was over and they scrambled out to the truck, pushing and shoving each other. The ride to town was slow until they came off the mountain and the road flattened out with tall cliffs on one side and the turquoise Caribbean on the other. They passed people walking with bundles balanced on their heads, taking produce to the market while the sprinkling rain formed a rainbow across their path.

"Boys! I have to go to the market. I'll drop you off at the comic store and pick you up later," Mary said, pulling to the side of the busy street.

They got out and ran across to Cee-Bee's, the only bookstore in town. Mary watched as they disappeared behind the swinging half-doors and knew they would be content to stay there for hours. She drove to the bay front and the open market and parked near the jetty, the same one she had landed on when she arrived on the island years before. She loved shopping in the market. It was an escape from the peace of the mountains and a time to re-live the vibrancy of the people.

She moved along the lines of women sitting on small benches, dressed in colorful garb and heads wrapped in vibrant cloth. Their faces lit up as she walked past them.

"Hello, Ma'am. Over here! I have some fresh fish today, and yams I get from de ground dis morning!" A large woman was pointing to the table in front of her.

"Hello, Anastasia, I'll get some fish on my way out, okay?"

"I'll be here waiting."

Her basket hung from her forearm as she walked down the aisles of friendly vendors.

"Ma'am! I have fresh lettuce and grapefruit," one called out to her and Mary walked over. "No thanks, Myra, but I do want some okra and callallou."

"Wait here and I go get it for you!" She was a short woman wearing a tired-looking straw hat. She had obvious seniority in the market and ran to other vendors and collected what Mary had requested. She came back minutes later and found Mary talking to a man who was selling meat.

"Okay, okay, I'll take two pounds, but only if it's fresh," Mary said.

"I just kill the cow a little while ago. You can't get it any fresher," the man said.

She laughed and pulled out five dollars. "How much?" She held it out.

"That's good Ma'am, here." He took the money and put the meat in her basket.

Myra handed her a paper bag. They talked briefly and Mary made her way back to her car, stopping to get some fish. She got in the truck and looked at the pack of Hillsborogh cigarettes left on the dashboard. The tobacco was grown and packaged on the island and it was the local favorite. She had never smoked before but without thinking, she picked up the pack and lit one, puffing cautiously and blowing the smoke out quickly. The taste was harsh but pleasant. She took another drag, and moved down the street with the cigarette hanging from her mouth. She parked and walked to the comic store and threw the cigarette into the gutter.

As she passed the Paz Hotel a voice came from inside

the bar. "Mary!" The swinging doors swung open and Hazel came running out.

"Do you have time for a quick drink?"

"Sure. The boys are buried in their comics and my throat is parched." She followed her into the small bar and sat at one of low metal tables. The place brought back a flood of memories.

"My God, Mary, you look terrific!" Hazel said, touching her arm and taking a swig on her beer.

"Thanks. I don't feel it," Mary said.

"What's wrong?"

"It's nothing. Just been a long day"

"So how are you doing up in the bush all by yourself?" Hazel said in her distinct English accent.

"It's fine," Mary said. "It does get lonely, but the boys keep me busy."

"Has Leo left?"

"There are no secrets on this island, are there?" Mary took a long swig of her beer.

"Not if you are one of the few white people on an island and there is only one small seaplane that comes once a week."

Mary took another swig.

"What you probably don't know is that he went to Barbados before he went up to the States," Hazel said.

"He did?" Mary set her glass on the table.

"You know he is seeing a woman there, don't you"

"Yes, you told me he was."

"That's a small island and like here, everyone knows what goes on. Hazel reached over and touched Mary's arm again, and squeezed it gently. "Word has it that Leo asked her to join him in the States."

Mary drank the rest of her beer quickly.

"I'm sorry," Hazel said.

"It's over with us anyway. I know divorce is a dirty word on the island, but that's what's happening." She pushed her chair back and they stood up together and embraced briefly.

"Thanks for the drink, I'll see you soon." She turned and walked out through the swinging doors.

She found the boys with their faces buried in comics sitting on the floor. They looked up when she came in.

"Hi Mum, can you buy these for us?" Ivan said, holding up *Batman, Superman*, and *Archie* comics.

"Sure. Let's go." She paid the man behind the table and they followed her out to the street. In a few minutes they were crossing the river and drove up the mountain, with the boys reading comics and Mary deep in thought.

CHAPTER **17**

"CAN YOU HEAR that?" Ivan spoke softly. It was a full moon and the boys were in bed.

"Yes, what is it?" Peter said. Without a word they moved to the windows and listened to the rhythmic sound of drums in the distance "I've heard that sound before. What do you think it is?

"Let's go find out," Ivan said softly, opening the window wide.

Barefoot and in pajamas, they jumped to the soft ground below. They rustled their way through the bush and down to their favorite hiding place in the bamboo. They stood in silence next to each other for several minutes before Peter touched Ivan's shoulder.

"Listen! It's coming from over there." He pointed down the hill.

The wind blew gently as the sound of drums and singing came through the thick brush, bringing the rhythm of the music with it. They moved out from the bamboo and followed the path down the hill until they came to the row of small homes where the laborers lived. They crept to the clearing in the back and looked out at the small crowd before them. The area was illuminated by "bouzeys" - bottles of kerosene with cloth wicks that produced dancing flames and thick clouds of black smoke. An open fire burned in the center of the group with a large pot resting on a circle of stones. The boys recognized LaLa the maid crouching next to it, adding wood to the blaze and stirring the pot. They stayed hidden under the leaves of the banana trees, watching the scene before them.

There were five men sitting together on small wooden benches - an accordion player, a man scraping an egg beater against a grater, another blowing into long hollow bamboo that produced a deep fog horn sound, and two others pounding on goat-skin drums. They sang out in sharp, guttural voices, and stomped their feet to a mesmerizing beat. Their eyes were closed and the fire reflected their sweating faces as they played in hypnotic rapture. The "jing-ping" band produced a distinctive brand of music, one the boys had heard before.

They watched spellbound as the four women started dancing around the fire, dressed in long colorful skirts and heads tied with bright cloth, their euphoric faces shimmering in the moonlight. They stomped their bare feet in the dirt, spinning circles around each other with their arms flailing as they danced in total abandonment. The men kept singing and playing, taking turns to gulp down jiggers of rum while the women danced. As they played on, the dancers appeared possessed in their dance of catharsis, in statements of resplendent emotional elimination; sweating, screaming, churning and swaying with eyes closed and arms open, braying out raspy Creole songs. Finally, LaLa fell to the ground and lay on her back, shaking violently, her skirt tightened around her legs as she rolled around and her body trembled. Suddenly, she was motionless, arms out-stretched, with eyes closed as if all life had left her, while the others kept dancing around her.

The music finally stopped and the dancers fell to the ground exhausted and writhing in ecstasy. The men grinned in approval and took more shots of rum. The two boys in the shadows looked at each other and without a word, got up and scrambled back up the path and through the trees, finally stopping beneath their bedroom window. They leaned a flat board against the house and crawled back up through the window and into their room, sliding back into their warm beds without a word between them. Peter lay on his back, breathing heavily and eyes wide open. The music kept throbbing through him and his mind raced for a meaning of the gripping spectacle. He thought about LaLa and her dancing and remembered a comment his mother had made about her voodoo.

The next morning they lay in their beds thinking about the night before and what the day might bring. "That was pretty cool what we saw last night, wasn't it." Peter said.

"Yeah, it was, a little weird, but very cool!" Ivan said. There was a long silence before he spoke again. "Hey! I have a great idea of something to do today! What would happen if we put some rum in the chicken water?"

Peter answered quickly. "What the hell are you talking about?"

"What would happen if we gave the chickens some rum?"

Peter sat up quickly. "I don't know but it could be fun to watch!" They jumped out of bed and ran to the kitchen. They hurried through breakfast and ran through the back door, grabbing a bottle of rum on the way out.

The chickens and roosters looked up at them from inside the henhouse and clucked loudly. Peter picked up the small sack of grain sitting in front of the wire gate, walked in and spread it on the ground.

"Wait!" Ivan said. "Let's not give them any water now so they will be really thirsty later. Then we can put the rum in the water and they will drink more of it!"

"Great idea!" They closed the wire door, leaving the water

dish empty, and with the rum stashed in the grass, they ran back to the house.

It was now late afternoon and they found the chickens walking around the empty water basin, clucking excitedly when the boys walked through the gate. Peter poured water from a watering can into the basin and Ivan topped it off with half a bottle of rum, then they quickly left and closed the gate behind them and sat on the grass outside to watch.

The thirsty chickens and roosters ran quickly to the basin, pushing and pecking each other to get their turn. There was silence, broken up by intermittent clucking. Suddenly the chickens looked up, cocking their heads sideways at the boys. The roosters kept drinking and then sat down quickly, and it wasn't long before the hens stood up and stumbled when they tried to walk. They rested on the ground and one got up and attempted to fly but crashed into the wire fence. The boys broke into fits of laughter as they watched the drunken chickens attempt to walk and fly, all the time clucking nervously.

"It reminds you of last night doesn't it?" Peter said, and they laughed out loud but stopped short when they heard their mother calling from below. They quickly emptied the chicken cocktail bowl and filled it with fresh water, closed the gate behind them, and ran towards the house unable to contain themselves. The questions came later when the chickens stopped laying eggs for two days and the boys had trouble keeping straight faces.

When Peter got the birthday gift of a small transistor radio, a new pastime evolved. The voices sounded alien, talking of things that they did not understand and playing music they had never heard before. The boys sat on the veranda at night, taking turns to listen to *The Voice of America*. When "rock and roll" came on, they got up and danced, giggling and shouting while Jumbie barked at the two little white boys dancing half naked in the moonlight.

The radio and an occasional *National Geographic* or *Life Magazine* gave the brothers glimpses of a different life in foreign lands, especially in America, the land their parents spoke of as "their first home." It was the birth of a dream that became the talk of "Some day when I go to America." When Penny came home for the holidays she told them how different life was on Barbados, which only intensified their dream. She was now old enough to spend most of the year at her boarding school and on holidays she often stayed with friends, which took the burden off Mary.

Their curiosity with the outside world was further aroused when the island got its first cinema. It was Saturday morning in town, and instead of reading comics, the boys walked to the Carib Cinema, eager to see their first movie. It was *The Coronation of the Queen,* a short documentary, followed by a cowboy musical *Seven Brides For Seven Brothers*. They came out ecstatic and Mary smiled all the way back home as they sang, "*Bless Your Beautiful Hide.*" It was several weeks before a new movie came, and when they saw *The Prisoner of Zenda,* the fencing saga with James Mason, it was all they needed to dive into another world of make-believe. This one brought constant challenges and duels with homemade swords, along with episodes of violence and blood, and a distraught mother who now cursed the day the movie theatre ever opened on the island.

CHAPTER **18**

THE SKY DARKENED suddenly, and the birds stopped sing-ing. Jumbie crawled under the bed, the cat disappeared, and the boys ran to their mother.

"I'll turn on the radio," Mary said. She listened intently to the crackling voice. "It's a hurricane. A bad one and it's almost upon us. Quick! Help me close up the house and get into the bedroom and lie on the floor next to the bed."

This was a drill they had been through only once before when they had experienced bad weather, but never the full force of a hurricane.

"I'm scared Mummy," said Peter, now lying on the floor. Mary was closing the shutters when the first powerful gust of wind slapped them back against the side of the house. The rain came quickly, bringing heavy sheets of water. Suddenly, their world turned upside down while they huddled on the floor and became lost in an eerie and foreboding reality. A large branch crashed onto the veranda and the house shud-dered as the boys curled up into tight balls. They listened to the screaming wind, the booming thunder, and the flashes of lightening that lit up the room long enough to see that the glass window had been shattered and the white curtains were being sucked up skyward. There was crashing of trees out-side and rain came pouring into the room. The boys began to cry with arms wrapped around their mother who was trying hard to stifle her own screams. Their world of shrieking terror seemed to last forever and they became paralyzed in time, never thinking about when it might end, only conscious of the very moment.

Suddenly, there was silence and they heard water pouring onto the floor, dripping off the drenched curtains and windowsill. Mary wrapped her arms around them and whispered, "It's over children. Everything is going to be all right."

After weeks of clean-up, the boys now counted the days to Christmas. Birthdays in September and November were non-events since there was no one to invite to parties, but Christmas had some significance. On the first day of December, the boys cut down a small tree, decorated it with cotton balls and tinfoil, and set it up next to the fireplace. Penny was home for the holidays and made comments about the tree, none of which the boys found amusing.

It was Christmas Eve and six men and three women arrived at the top of the marble steps, carrying their "bouzies" which lit up their faces in a smoky, eerie fashion, and they began singing Christmas carols. They brought with them "Batons" or "bamboo cannons" and set them up while Mary passed around shots of rum in small tin cups. The cannons were hollowed-out bamboo sleeves and when kerosene was poured at one end and lit through a small hole in the side, the resulting blasts were deafening, and the boys laughed and covered their ears. Mary kept filling the carolers' cups and they kept singing their versions of Jingle Bells and White Christmas. The outdoor concert finally ended when the rum ran out and the drunken carolers had difficulty singing and operating their cannons.

"Thank you," Mary said. "No more tonight. The children have to go to bed."

"Yes, Ma'am. We go leave now. You have any more rum?"

"No more, good night."

"Okay, Ma'am, we go now."

The boys watched them leave, singing and stumbling, as they made their way back down the road, followed by trails of smoke from their bottle torches.

They woke up early the next day and rushed to count the gifts, making enough noise to wake their mother and sister. The unwrapping went quickly, and they soon ran off to play with their new discoveries. It was their favorite day except for the silent regret over the absence of their father.

They spent the afternoon in some new clothes, playing hide and seek in the tall grass. Now Peter broke out of the bushes, trying to escape from his enraged brother who had been hit in the chest by a Citronella grass arrow. When pulled out by the stem, the grass made an excellent weapon when thrown like a javelin, travelling for yards with uncanny accuracy. This game ended abruptly when his arrow met its mark and Peter made a hasty retreat. His thirst was overwhelming as he raced towards the house, threw open the kitchen door, and turned on the faucet for water. A rusty trickle fell into his hands and he remembered that a tree had recently fallen on the pipe that brought water to the house from the mountain spring. He searched frantically for some water, and grabbed a bottle from the pantry shelf, raised it to his mouth, and guzzled the clear liquid, almost emptying the bottle. He suddenly grabbed his throat, doubled over, and started retching, and the sickening taste of kerosene came back up his mouth and through his nose. He gave a guttural cough and a desperate cry for help and staggered into the kitchen. He sank to his knees and kept trying to vomit out the foul taste. He fell forward, hitting his head against the bench and onto the floor. It was there that Viola found him unconscious.

The doctor arrived an hour later and soberly informed Mary that after ingesting almost a quart of kerosene, there was little chance of survival. He said it would be useless trying to transport him to the hospital, which was an hour away and had no facilities to deal with this kind of emergency at such a progressive stage. He was "Terribly sorry" but now the matter was "In God's hands." He left the house and promised to call the next day.

LaLa came into the room barefoot and approached the bed. Her penetrating eyes looked down on the boy who lay with a blanched, angelic expression on his face. She turned and asked Mary to leave the room for a few moments.

"Why?" Mary asked. Her face was streaked with tears.

"Ma'am, dis here is serious business. I will make him come back."

Without a word of protest, Mary motioned to Ivan to follow her as she walked out of the room.

LaLa bent over Peter and touched his forehead with her sweaty palm. Her chanting was a whisper, and then a monotone mantra. With hands outstretched and palms down, she continued her murmur, and her body began to tremble. She knelt on the floor next to the bed, and an ominous silence filled the room.

Peter's consciousness came slowly into focus, and he felt that he was rising up from his body, like steam from a simmering kettle. The sound of Lala's chanting came up to him and he felt himself floating, hovering over his own body. He was looking down at himself, watching the scene below him as the "voodoo woman" performed her ritual. He saw Jumbie lying on the floor and Viola kneeling next to him. Minutes later, Ivan and Mary walked back into the room and stood over him, her arms clutching her stomach as she stared at LaLa who was still kneeling, swaying back and forth. With trembling hands, Mary leaned over and put her face next to his, searching for a breath.

LaLa said softly. "Just wait Ma'am, he coming back."

Peter felt himself drifting down towards his body, as if riding on a cloud. He came to rest and now her voice was clearer.

"Master Peter, come back home," she said.

He became conscious and could feel his eyes open, breaking through the built-up crust. He saw filtered light through the cracks in LaLa's fingers covering his face, and could smell the patchouli oil on her warm palms. She lifted them off and he looked up into her eyes and she gave a slight nod, acknowledging his return. He felt a long tongue against his face as Jumbie put her paws on the bed next to him and whimpered in his ear.

Mary's mouth fell open and she clasped his cold hands in her own. She looked at LaLa. "I don't understand. What did you do?"

"It no matter, Ma'am. Your boy is fine. It was not his time." LaLa straightened her back, and walked out of the room with remnants of a trance on her face.

In the days that followed Mary never looked for an explanation from LaLa. Voodoo or not, she just accepted the experience.

Peter was back on his feet in two days, and now he and Ivan broke out of the dense underbrush from the small path and onto the main road where they waited for Christian, their hunting companion. Half naked and barefoot, with sinewy bodies and long disheveled hair, they shouted to their friend to catch up with them. Christian had worked on the estate since they were infants. He was "the boiler man" whose job had been to keep the boiler stoked with wood to distill the large copper container of citronella grass. Now that the estate had shut down, his purpose was that of caretaker and gardener.

They watched as he emerged from the brush. Wearing only a tattered pair of shorts, his muscular body glistened with sweat and rain, and his large chest heaved from exertion. He was a short man of huge stature with deep-set eyes over a broad nose and dark skin, pot-marked from the years in front of the hot boiler.

He was whistling as he walked towards them, something he did constantly, which made him always easy to find. He found humor in everything, and his laugh was infectious. The two dogs sat at their heels with their tongues hanging out, panting from the heat and exertion of the day's adventure.

The .22 caliber rifles were strapped to their backs, with homemade slingshots hanging around their necks. The slingshots had less range than the guns but were just as accurate, and much preferred, since ammunition was free. Hanging next to the slingshots against their chests and backs was their catch for the day – necklaces of dead birds strung together. The boys were oblivious of the blood dripping down their bodies and the feathers sticking to their sweaty skin. Their guns, slingshots and bloody birds adorned their bodies as they stood laughing on the lonely road, peeling oranges with long knives. A misty rain cooled them off as they stuffed the oranges in their mouths and joked with Christian about the fresh meat they now had for the dinner.

The sound of an approaching car caused them to stop and listen. It was not a road traversed by many cars and now the small taxi appeared around the corner, slowed down, and stopped in front of the threesome. Jimmy, the local taxi driver grinned up at them.

"Hey fellas, what's happening?" he said.

Without answering, they stooped down to look in the back seat at the two very white faces - tourists with cameras in hand and obvious shock on their faces at what they saw. The overweight woman opened her mouth to say something but nothing came out. The boys kept staring at them and quickly looked at each other and winked. They pulled out their knives and put them between their teeth, their eyes narrowed and they growled menacingly, moving towards the open car windows. Christian quickly joined in, opened his eyes wide and snorted loudly as he raised his huge arms up high, glaring down at the terrified visitors.

The woman screamed first and the bald man clutched her, now both the color of sheets. Jimmy shouted some patois curse words, slammed his car into gear and lurched forward. As it gained speed up the narrow road, the boys chased it, with sweat and bird blood dripping down their bodies, waving knives and guns at the terrified foreigners. They watched the two white faces with mouths open through the back window and saw Jimmy's fist shaking out the side, as the straining car quickly disappeared around the corner. There was a momentary silence and the three looked at each other, heaving from the exertion, then quickly broke into hysterical laughter. The dog barked and warm raindrops fell over their bodies, washing away the blood and dirt.

CHAPTER 19

WHEN LEO ARRIVED unexpectedly, the boys were thrilled to see him but devastated when he said he would be leaving again in a few days. His conversation with Mary was unemotional until he said he might send his mother Maria to live on the estate.

"What? Your mother is almost eighty years old and you said the reason you went back to the States was to be with her since she was now alone. So what do you mean you are sending her down here? Who the hell do you think will look after her? Me? Forget it! I'm moving to town."

"What will you do in town?"

"Never mind that. I'll survive. I'll find a job. I am not staying here. This place is no longer a home for the boys and me. If you send her down she will have to live here by herself." She continued, "Tell me Leo, will you send money to help with the children?"

"I'll do what I can," he said.

"Do what you can? Leo, for Christ's sake, you're the one who brought me down here with a wild dream and the promise of a wonderful life, and you made it into a prison for yourself. You choose to abandon the family, have an affair with someone, divorce me and return to New York and now you're saying you're going to send your mother down here? Why? To abandon her too? Didn't you learn anything from your parents?" She was shaking with a rage she had not felt for some time.

"What the hell do you mean by that? You didn't know my parents so shut up!"

She looked directly into his eyes and said quietly, "And neither did you, Leo." He stared at her and then turned and walked out the door.

That night was a frightening one for the boys. Leo had been drinking before he made his way into the bedroom where Mary was waiting. The boys sat up in their beds and listened to the fighting and sobbing behind closed doors.

Mary's voice rang out above the shouting. "Damn you, Leo, why do you give up and abandon everything?"

"What are you talking about? I just need to get away from here."

"Think about it, your job, your dreams, your own children and me, and now your mother. Does that sound like abandonment?" Mary's voice got louder. "I know you think your parents abandoned you, but it was you who abandoned them! Your father was a hero but you didn't understand him and so you gave up on him. Is this some form of revenge?" She was breathing heavily, uncertain if she had gone too far, and yet her anger let the words flow

The boys sat on their beds, looking at each other's profile in the dark. Outside, the rain started beating against the windows, muffling the angry words, and they could hear the sounds of sobbing, and their hearts sank in fear.

There was a knock at their door, and without a word, they quickly opened their windows and squeezed out, jumping to the ground below where they stood close to each other, feeling the rain against their faces. It was an exercise they had been through before, and now they turned and ran barefoot through the bushes and took refuge in the Still House. They lay close to each other on bags of fertilizer, listening to the storm outside, too frightened to cry, and too uncomfortable to sleep.

It was several hours before the rain stopped. Now covered in mosquito bites, they made their way back up to the house, climbed up through the window and into their room where they stripped off their wet pajamas and slipped naked into their warm beds.

For the next two days the boys watched from a distance as their father packed his suitcases. His farewell was cursory and without emotion, and this time they knew he was not coming back. "Goodbye boys, I hope to see you soon," He said, and got into the small truck and drove away. Viola and Lala were standing under the trees, watching silently.

The boys ran to their mother who was sitting on the veranda, staring at the valley below.

"Daddy's gone," Peter said.

"Yes, I know," she replied glumly. "Come here, I want to talk to you."

They walked over and sat in the chairs next to her. She had a calm expression on her face. "Boys, your father has left again and I don't know when he will be back. In the meantime, we will stay here and then move into town. Since you both started school, it has been very difficult driving you back and forth four days a week so I will find work in town and a place to live. Your grandmother may be coming down from America and will be living here. Viola is going to look after her but Lala is going back to her village. Everything is going to be fine and I am sure you will like living in town."

The boys stared at her with quizzical looks on their faces. "We're going to live in town?" asked Peter.

"Yes, I don't know where yet, but I will find something."

The boys looked at each other with mouths open. "That will be so cool," Ivan said.

CHAPTER 20

THEY STOOD IN their new home, feeling the intense heat from the sloping galvanize roof above their heads. Mary inspected the tiny room that was now hers and felt a deep disappointment in the accommodations, but relieved that at least she now had a place to live. She felt belittled by her drop in stature from being the mistress of a sprawling estate to living in the attic of an old hotel, but without many options, she quickly accepted the position of manager.

One of the oldest structures in the town with a red roof, a large veranda, and brightly colored shutters that surrounded the building, the Paz Hotel had only twelve small guest rooms. By midday the heat forced guests to retreat to the veranda and small restaurant and bar on the street level which was busy with locals and tourists. It was also a favorite hangout for the local "wabines" which was explained to the boys as "women who did their business at night."

The boys started at the local Grammar School where they were two of the few white faces and quickly became a curious novelty for their classmates. Without any experience in formal schooling, their lack of certain "social skills" caused some turmoil at the school, which had a policy of strict discipline, and the boys often found themselves in the headmaster's office, trying to explain their antics.

"Listen, here! You can't just take your shoe off and throw it at another boy," Mr. Archer the headmaster said sternly, as he grabbed Peter by the neck and led him to his desk.

"But he was laughing at me!"

"First of all, you address me as 'Sir' at all times, and secondly, I don't care if he laughed at you. You don't throw your shoe at him! Did you know you cut his lip?" Mr. Archer asked.

"Good. I'm glad," Peter responded impetuously.

"Bend over!" Mr. Archer shouted and Peter grabbed the side of his desk and waited for his punishment. The ritual of "caning" was somewhat analogous to flogging on a pirate ship where the student held on to the desk and was beat on the buttocks with a long wooden rod. The number of lashes depended on the nature of the crime, and Mr. Archer's mood. The exercise brought screams heard throughout the school, which was enjoyed by the rest of the student body. It didn't take many of these beatings before the boys learned to put a small towel in their pants when they dressed for school in the event they had to pay a visit to Mr. Archer that day. With the same expressions of pain on their faces and the rehearsed histrionics, Mr. Archer became none the wiser. The canings also decreased in frequency as the boys quickly learned some new standards of acceptable behavior and settled into their first year.

The mornings initiated a hurried departure from the hotel attic as the stillness of the air and the ominous tropical sun beat down mercilessly, turning it into a hotbox. At the end of the day, they did their homework downstairs until sundown when the heat dissipated. As night descended on the town, the noise from the street below became more acute, and when the movie theater across the street began its nightly show, the sound carried directly into their bedroom. The incessant noise of the day and night was a hard adjustment for the family to make after the serenity of their country living.

It wasn't long before the boys discovered that half way through the movie, when the large windows of the cinema were opened, they could sit and watch the rest of movie, albeit with only half a screen, which they did most nights after Mary went to bed. She did not realize the impact the cinema was having on them until she overheard some of the language they were repeating, and realized they were getting their first dose of sexual education directly from Hollywood.

The onus of raising the boys in town was taking its toll on Mary and she desperately wanted something better for the three of them. After the first year, she moved Peter to the Saint Mary's Academy, run by the Christian Brothers, and kept Ivan at the Grammar School. She believed that separated, they would be less prone to trouble, and the experience would be beneficial for both of them. They had been inseparable all their lives and she wanted to give them the opportunity to follow their own path.

At Saint Mary's Peter was one of two white students in the school of two hundred boys. The Christian Brothers were Americans and the school was new, an experiment by the Catholic Church in an attempt to educate the youth of this tropical island. The Brothers were kind and dedicated teachers that took a "no nonsense" approach, and they soon realized that this white boy was intelligent, and as the only non-catholic, a potential convert.

The required uniform was short pants, a clean white shirt with a blue and gold striped tie, long socks and polished brown shoes, and this was a challenge for Peter who had trouble keeping it all clean. The school taught him how to study, and the importance of prayer, hard work, and discipline. At the first sign of unruliness, the Brother would move hastily down the aisle between the desks and grab him by the shirt, pick him up off his feet, and after a momentary cessation in breathing, he was shoved back into his seat. These episodes were very effective, and Peter quickly conformed to the schools policy of discipline, which was vastly different from that of the Grammar School. He learned to respect others, and although his color was not an issue, he felt guilty that he was not a Catholic. He prayed at the beginning and end of each day, and before and after each class. The Hail Mary's, Lord's Prayer, and Acts of Contrition rolled off his tongue, and he felt he was having a constant conversation with God. Back at their space in the hotel attic, he asked his mother if he could keep a statue of the Virgin Mary in his bedroom.

"Why?" she asked.

"So I can pray to her at night," he said.

"Peter, I don't believe one religion is better than the other, and yet I want you to learn the importance of belief and faith. If the Virgin Mary will help you get that, she can be in your room with you."

"Thanks, Mummy. I believe in her and she will be good company."

Mary saw it as another step forward in the boy's adolescence. Ivan however, kept questioning the purpose of a statue of a strange looking white woman under the table in his bedroom.

Homework was a challenging time of the day and done in the back room off the bar, the only cool part of the hotel in the afternoon. The boys found it hard not to listen to the drunken gossip of the locals, the rowdiness of the occasional sailors, and the enchantment of the local prostitutes trying to drum up business. When bored and business was slow, the girls would look over to the boys and wave. Peter's favorite was a very pretty, charcoal-skinned girl who would often sit by his side and watch him as he wrote in his notebooks.

"You one lucky boy, you know." Her features were stunning, with auburn skin, gray eyes, and soft black curly hair. Salina was a Carib, the Indian tribe that was an integral part of the island's history. The remaining Caribs now lived in the interior of the island on their own reservation and for the most part, they kept to themselves. With limited opportunity on the reservation, young Caribs were often sent out to mix with the locals and seek employment in the towns and villages. Salina capitalized on her beauty to become a prostitute, and when the ships were in, she was the most popular.

"Why do you say that?"

"Because I can't read or write."

"You can't? Why not?"

"Because I never went to school. My village didn't have a school, and when I left home, I came to work in town, I couldn't get a job, so now I work the streets"

"What exactly do you do with these men?" Peter leaned forward as he lowered his voice.

She reached over and ruffled his hair. "Never mind dat, maybe I show you in a few years."

"Why not now?" Peter asked with a smile.

She gave a short laugh. Just then the bar doors swung open and two white men walked in, speaking German. A ship had come in that morning which meant business for her. She got up from the table and wiggled a finger at him "You know what? You too bad for your age," she said, giving him his favorite smile. She moved quickly to the bar, swaying her rear end as she walked over and put her arms around the two sailors. Peter looked after her, picked up his books and ran up the steep wooden stairs to the attic.

On nights that were especially hot and humid, the boys crept downstairs and out to the narrow streets to explore. They made friends with what Mary had referred to as "bad elements" that lived in the shanties near the hotel. On several occasions, the boys followed them through town and watch them break into park cars and steal. They witnessed fights and heard language that frightened them, and when Peter suffered a cut from a thrown bottle, they realized that these relationships were dangerous, and that staying at the hotel and reading a book or watching the movies through half-open windows was a safer pastime.

It became painfully obvious to Mary that she couldn't continue living at the Paz, and she begun to search for a change. She had been offered the position of manager of the local Cooperative Bank, which she accepted, and quickly started looking for a new home. She confided in Hazel who had become a close friend, and who helped her look for a solution when suddenly Hazel's life turned upside down. Her husband died instantly from what appeared to be an accidental gun shot, an act that was never fully explained to the boys. The sadness and turmoil of his death was soon overshadowed when Hazel offered to have Mary and the boys move in with her just fifteen minutes out of town. Hazel's children were older and living overseas and she was now alone in the large house on the top of a steep hill, which captured beautiful vistas of the town and harbor below.

It was a dream come true for the family. Mary and Hazel shared the master bedroom, and the boys had separate rooms, a novelty which thrilled them. Below Peter's bedroom window, there was a small house for Evelyn the maid and her son Ray, who quickly became a close friend, play-mate, and companion troublemaker. Their new home was a perfect fit and Mary was overwhelmed by the impact of her good fortune. It was a refreshing change from living in the hotel, and it brought a semblance of sanity to the family.

CHAPTER 21

MARIA ARRIVING BY BOAT MID AUGUST. PLEASE MEET.

Mary's hand trembled in anger as she read the telegram from Leo. She couldn't believe that he was sending his mother to live on the island. As she pondered the options, she knew there was nothing else to do except get her settled on the estate where she would have to be alone. She shuddered at the thought of Leo's act of inconsideration.

The boys watched as the small motor vessel pulled up to the wooden jetty, arriving from the neighboring island of Martinique, where Maria flew in from New York. They watched as an old woman in a light dress and wide-brimmed hat was helped onto the jetty. She stood and surveyed everything around her and her eyes settled on Mary and the two scruffy looking boys that now approached her.

"Mary, what a pleasure to see you. Where is Leo?" Her voice was light.

"Welcome, Maria. Leo said he was unable to make it. Here, let me help you." Mary picked up the small suitcase as two men passed several bags from the boat on to the jetty.

"Ma'am, where do you want these?" one of them asked.

"Take them to the small truck, and this is for you." Mary handed him some coins.

"Thank you, Ma'am" he said with a grin.

Mary motioned for the two boys to step forward. "Maria, this is Ivan and Peter, your grandsons".

Maria looked down at them and held out her hand. "My goodness, you boys are grown! I never expected this."

She looked over at Mary, shading her eyes from the sun "What do you mean Leo wasn't able to make it? He said he would be here."

"He did? Well, he asked me to meet you and show you around. He gave no indication when he might be here."

"That's very disappointing," Maria said.

They drove up the mountain to the estate and Maria stared at the wild outdoors. The boys ran off looking for Jumbie who came crashing through the bushes. They ran into their room while Mary showed Maria her bedroom and introduced her to Viola.

"Maria, I need to go now. Viola will take care of you and we will come to visit ."

"Do you really have to leave?"

"I don't live here anymore. Sorry, but I have to go."

"Very well, then. Thank you and please do come see me." She gave Mary and the boys hugs.

Mary drove off, trying hard to restrain her anger.

In the days and weeks that followed, she visited Maria several times, bringing books and groceries. There was a piano at the house, which Leo had acquired years earlier, and Maria was thrilled to find it at the house.

Arrangements were made for Viola to have groceries brought up every week. Christian was the only laborer left on the estate and lived in the same small house down the hill. His meager living came from his garden -- two acres of hillside where he grew vegetables and bananas, some of which he gave to Maria, and the rest he sold in the market.

It had been three weeks since Mary had last seen Maria and now she drove up, consumed in thought. The memories of her life on the estate ran rampant with every visit. She thought of Maria as a wonderful, talented woman who had been cut off from living out her passion for music and culture, which she loved so much. Maybe she can teach the little Tarzans something about the world, Mary thought, as she turned the last corner and parked. She found Maria stooped over in her garden.

Maria put down her garden shovel. "Look at this wonderful garden! I should have some carrots any day now."

"That's great, Maria. Where did you ever learn how to garden?"

"With some help from Christian. One has to make the most out of what they have to work with, and there is obviously not much else here."

"How are you doing?" Mary asked.

"I'm fine. Any word from Leo?" she asked wiping her forehead.

"I haven't heard from him. I thought he might have written to you."

"Not a word. How would I have gotten a letter up here anyway?" The old woman looked down to the ground. "Not a word," she repeated.

"Maria, I know it must be lonely up here for you so I thought you might want the boys to visit you on the weekends. They can get a ride with Mr. Ford who lives up the road and go back with him on Monday to school. Would you like that?"

"That's great, but what will they do up here for two days? I can't drive and I have heard from Viola that they are a little wild. I can't supervise them."

"You shouldn't have to. They are older now and remember, this is where they grew up, so they will find plenty to do, and it will be company for you. Maybe you can teach them to play the piano?" Mary said.

"What a great idea, although this piano is badly out of tune,"

"You think they know that?" Mary said, and Maria giggled.

For their first planned weekend visit, Mary had arranged to have the boys wait after school in front of The Paz for a ride with Mr. Ford, an American who had a small office in town selling outboard engines. He worked until five every evening when he retired to The Paz for several drinks before leaving in his Morris Minor. The boys got out of school at four and waited outside. They were tired, hot, and hungry when they climbed into his tiny car that evening. Ivan sat in the front and Peter stuffed himself into the back with a small bag and a box of groceries. At the first corner, Ivan turned to look back at Peter with wide eyes.

Mr. Ford belched and the odor of rum and beer filled the car as he swerved to avoid hitting a woman crossing the street. They moved up the narrow road, the weak headlamps lighting only a few feet ahead of them. Suddenly, Mr. Ford pulled over under a large tree, stumbled out of the car and started urinating. The car started to roll backwards and Ivan pulled up the handbrake in time to stop it from going into the valley below while Mr. Ford came running back, peeing on his leg.

"We can walk from here," Ivan said.

"No. I'll get you to the bottom of your road just a little further up." They were his first words since they had left town. After the final sharp turn, he came to a stop at the unpaved road and looked at his two sweating passengers.

"Do you want me to take you up?"

The boys exchanged glances and quickly got out. "No, that's all right. Thank you." The car jerked forward, backfiring as it rounded the first turn.

"Jesus Christ! I can't believe we made it!" Ivan said, looking up at the faint outline of the road that would take them up to the estate.

The rising moon helped them along until they reached the dark house. Ravenous, they sat on the bench in the kitchen and by the light of a flashlight, quickly devoured a can of sardines with some bread, and washed it down with water.

Peter wiped his mouth on his shirt. "That's it?" he said, watching Ivan looking in the half empty box of groceries.

"Nothing we don't have to cook."

"God damn it! I'm starving!"

"Let's go to bed," Ivan said.

They made their way down the open hallway to their room, careful not to wake their grandmother. It had been a long time since they had slept in their beds and nothing had changed. They quickly slipped under the thin blankets, smelling of sardines and breathing heavily as they listened to a new family of rats that had settled in the attic above them.

Maria - Granny

L'imprevue House

CHAPTER **22**

DAYBREAK BROUGHT SUNLIGHT pouring through the windows, the sound of a distant rooster, and a whining dog outside.

"It's Jumbie!" Peter pounced out of bed and ran to the door. Now thinner and older, the dog whimpered with joy.

Granny appeared in the doorway. "Hello boys, it's good to see you. After breakfast let's start your lessons, shall we?

The boys exchanged quick glances. "Lessons?" Ivan said.

"Your mother didn't tell you? I'm going to give you piano lessons when you are here every weekend. Won't that be great?"

There was a momentary silence. "How long will they take?" asked Peter.

"An hour each. Go have some breakfast and I'll see you at the piano in half an hour." She turned and walked down the open hallway.

"Damn it! Piano lessons?" Ivan said.

"I don't know, learning to play the piano sounds pretty cool."

"You go first and let me know how it is."

Peter put on a shirt and washed his hands, and walked down the open hall. They ate a breakfast of cold porridge and hardboiled eggs, and Viola walked into the room. She looked older but still the same smile.

"Hello Viola. I'm glad you're here. I love your cooking."

"I am glad to see you. I go make you boys fat every weekend." They laughed and she sauntered back into the kitchen.

The sound of piano music came from the next room and Peter got up and walked to the door. "Granny?"

She looked at him, and patted the bench next to her "Please, come sit here."

Peter stared at the keys before him. "Before we start," Maria said softly. "I want you to learn to give me your full attention. I will only see you on the weekends, so I want you to take your time and focus on the lesson. Do you understand?"

"Yes, Granny." He said looking up at her piercing blue eyes, wondering what he was getting himself into.

She introduced him to the notes on the keyboard, playing one at a time. She then worked with simple scales, humming the notes as she played them.

"Focus on the sound each one makes," she said. "Think of nothing else for that moment." She pressed one key and let the sound linger before she hit the next one.

Peter lost track of time and became captivated by the old woman next to him. She came from a world that excited him, and he wanted to learn more.

The weekend visits with Granny continued despite the frightening ride up. The boys enjoyed being on their own and Peter looked forward to learning more from his grandmother, and about his grandfather Ivan, whom she had spoke about. This was the tale that excited him the most.

The lesson was over and he closed the thin music book in front of him. "Granny, you said Grandpa was put in jail and he escaped. Why was he put in jail?"

"He was jailed by the Czar who didn't like his writings."

"What is a Czar and where exactly is Russia? And if you are my father's mother, does that mean that I am part Russian?"

"That's a good question," she said. "The Czar was the leader of Russia which is a country on the other side of the world, and yes, it does mean that you are part Russian. It also means that you are the grandson of a great man who helped change the course of history."

Peter brushed his hair from his eyes. "How exactly did he do that?"

"Your grandfather was a writer who wrote about the leaders of Russia and how the people were not given any freedom, and that they should revolt against the Czar. That is why he was put in prison. However, he had planted a seed in the minds of the people and they started to believe that freedom was possible. He was a very important part of the Russian Revolution." She paused and looked at him.

"What's a revolution?"

"It's when the people of a country are starving for freedom and they rise up against their leaders. They revolt, and many lives are lost in the process, but in the end, they get their freedom. Does that make sense to you?"

Peter's eyes were now open wide. "I think so. I'm not sure I understand what it's like to live without freedom, but tell me, how did Grandpa escape from prison?"

"Next time. It's a long story and you go back to school tomorrow so let's talk again next weekend. Now run along and play. Tell Ivan I'm not feeling well and he doesn't have to have a lesson today. I am sure he won't mind."

Peter nodded and slid off the bench. "Thanks, Granny."

He found Ivan in the bedroom sitting on the floor building a kite. "Hey, Ivan, you don't have to go for a lesson. Granny said it's okay."

"That's great," he said. "Hey, help me with this kite. I want to have another kite war. Finish yours. I think all you need is a tail."

Peter looked down at his kite on the floor, made out of red tissue paper and thin sticks from coconut branches fastened together with strips of paper and a paste of flour and water. He got down on his knees and finished working on it, engrossed in thoughts of his grandfather. Moments later, he picked up his kite and admired his handiwork. "Let's go," he said, grabbing his .22 rifle from under his bed. Ivan did the same and they ran outside to the back of the house and used a ladder to climb onto the roof with kites and rifles in hand.

The game was simple. Each boy would take up a position on either end of the roof, get their kites into the sky as high as possible and when the word was given, they would start firing at the opponent's kite. The first kite to break loose or hit the ground was the loser. Rapid fire from Ivan caused Peter's kite to take a dive but not before Peter kept firing at Ivan's which quickly broke loose. The game, like all the ones in the past, ended with a barrage of accusations. Empty bullet shells hurled at each other. Fists started flying and the boys rolled off the roof and fell into the yard below.

The screams brought Granny out of her room and onto the veranda carrying a long broom, which she swung madly at the wrestlers until they rolled away into the bushes. Now scratched and bloody, they looked up at her and smiled -- an old woman with long grey hair, standing on the veranda with a broom and screaming in a foreign language.

CHAPTER **23**

PETER ARRIVED AT school when the bell rang. He felt safe there and had begun to feel a trust in the Brothers that he had not experienced from other teachers, and became especially attached to Brother Gorman, a large, red-haired Irishman. Peter relished the special attention he got from him, but was concerned when he overheard a conversation coming from the principal's office.

"I don't know what you see in that boy and I don't think he can last here, he's too wild. I don't know how you can tame him. He's like a caged animal, and not even Catholic!"

"I can do it. He just needs guidance." Brother Gorman said.

"Okay, he's all yours. At least convert him will you? He will be lost without the Lord's help."

"I will do my best."

Peter smiled as he walked back to his classroom, rubbing his knuckles where his math teacher had just smacked him with a heavy ruler.

Class was over and they all stood and recited a litany of prayers - three Hail Marys, two Our Fathers and An Act Of Contrition. He was walking out and Brother Gorman motioned to him.

"Sit down, Peter. I want to talk to you."

He sat quickly on the bench. "Yes Brother?"

"I want you to know that I think you are a good student

and you could be the best student in the class." He loosened the collar of his robe.

"You do?"

"Yes, but you are easily distracted and in your desire for attention, you disrupt the whole class, and that is not acceptable."

Peter was silent. He stared at his teacher, realizing for the first time that they had the same color eyes.

"Listen to me. You need to learn to focus on the present moment and nothing else, and stop disturbing the other students. Do you understand what I am saying?

Peter nodded slowly. "Yes, Brother."

"Good. Remember what I have said. Now go, and may the Lord go with you."

Peter stood up and walked outside to join the rest of the students shuffling out the large iron gates. His mind was on what the Brother had said which reminded him of what his grandmother kept telling him at the piano - focus on the notes and just listen. He walked past the Catholic Church and headed downtown, oblivious of the surrounding chatter, the honking horns, and slow moving cars. He stopped to buy a "Frozen Joy" - ice cubes made out of fresh guava juice -- and dug into his pocket and handed his favorite lady vendor a copper penny.

It was Friday and he walked towards The Paz for his ride up to Granny. "I take it he's inside?" He said to Ivan, who was sitting on the curb.

"Yeah, and don't worry, he wasn't waiting for you."

Peter pushed the swinging doors open and Mr. Ford turned, annoyed at the distraction while Peter looked for his favorite girl Salina, but she was nowhere to be seen.

"Wait outside," Mr. Ford said with a wave of his hand as

he gulped down his drink and laughed with the three other blurry-eyed men.

It was seven o'clock when he finally pushed open the doors and the boys were talking to Jimmy the taxi driver, joking about their antics a couple years before on the mountain road.

"Okay, climb in," Mr. Ford said, bumping into the fender. The boys exchanged worried glances.

"Shit!" Peter said under his breath, "Here we go again!" Jimmy was shaking his head as they lay their small bag and groceries on the back seat.

The car moved slowly through the narrow streets before crossing the bridge out of town. The speed increased and the boys tightened their grips on the door handles while the driver belched and shifted gears to start the climb up the mountain.

Two miles from their drop off, he turned suddenly into the driveway of a home the boys knew where a white woman lived. They had seen her around town and nicknamed her "The Batwoman" because of her pasty white skin, long black hair, and small beady eyes. Her strange appearance gained her the name they had gleaned from their Batman comics.

"Why are we stopping here?" Ivan asked quickly.

"I'll be right back. You boys wait in the car." Mr. Ford said as he parked under a large tree and pulled himself out of the car. They watched him walk up to the door and be greeted by the Batwoman. She threw her arms around him and he quickly tried to get her inside, wanting to avoid the scrutiny of his waiting passengers.

"What the hell?" said Peter.

They sat with the car doors open, listening to the sounds of the crickets and night frogs all around them. When he appeared an hour later it was dark and the boys were tired and hungry.

"Sorry about the delay," he said gruffly. He put the car into gear and it shot forward up the hill.

At the bottom of the road the boys got out quickly and slammed the door. It was a long walk up the rough road and very late when they got to the house. This time there wasn't even the luxury of a sardine dinner before they fell into their beds exhausted.

Next morning , after some porridge and eggs, Peter walked into the room where Granny was playing softly with her eyes closed. She looked up at him, moved over, and patted the space next to her.

An hour later she folded her music and smiled. "You did well today."

"Granny?"

"Yes?"

"How did Grandpa escape from prison? You said you would tell me."

She looked at him and after a moment, said softly, "With the help of a bird."

Peter squinted at her. "A bird?"

"Yes, a dove." She took a sip of water from her glass, and sitting on the piano bench, she relayed the story of Ivan's escape up to the time when he got on the boat bound for America.

"That's an incredible story," Peter said, with eyes wide.

"Yes, and it's all true." She patted him on the shoulder and got up, leaving him sitting at the piano.

Now the boys moved noiselessly through the thick forest, shooting "Perdui" and "Peepeerite," birds that tasted delicious when fried over hot coals. Several hours went by and they had traversed the thick jungle and were now tired and thirsty. Sitting on a fallen tree branch with a string of dead birds around their necks, they peeled grapefruit and devoured them, while Jumbie lay panting at their feet

"Hey Ivan, has Granny told you the story about Grandpa?" Peter spat out a seed.

"What story?" Ivan asked.

"The one about him in prison and how he escaped."

"I knew he went to prison for something but never found out how he escaped. When I'm done with the lesson I just want to get out of there." He put a stone in his slingshot and took aim at a branch, hitting the target.

"It is such a cool story. "Do you know he was saved by a dove?"

"Bullshit. How?"

Sitting in the middle of the virgin forest, with sunlight streaming through the tops of the tall trees, Peter did his best to relay the story of their grandfather.

"Man, that's incredible. Did you just make that up?" Ivan asked.

"Do you really think I could make something like that up?"

"Do you think it's true?"

"I'm sure it is. Now I feel bad we're shooting birds, if one really saved his life," Peter said.

"You're bullshitting, right? You want to eat? I'm sure he thought of eating that bird many times before he let it go."

"You're probably right. But think about it, if he had eaten it, we wouldn't be here right now."

"You have a point there. Now let's go and cook them." Ivan said, standing up.

Peter grabbed his gun, wiped the blood from his chest, and followed his brother along the self-made path.

Back at the house they sat at the small square table in

two large stuffed chairs to play poker while Viola was pluck-
ing and cleaning the birds for dinner. Outside, the sky lit up
with a brilliant flashes of lightening, followed by the booming
of thunder before the rain began cascading against the glass
windows. They didn't talk much and played for an hour until
Ivan accused him of cheating, and tempers flared.

Peter turned to look through the window and turned back
at his smirking brother. "Hey, let's get our water pistols and if
one of us is caught cheating he gets squirted in the eye."

"Great idea!" Ivan said, and they ran out of the room.

They both came back to the table shirtless, looked at each
other and laughed, and Peter quickly dealt the cards.

It wasn't long before they were dripping wet and laughing at each other while they explored more innovative ways
of cheating. Suddenly a clap of thunder shook the house and
without a word between them, they pushed their chairs back
and ran outside, followed closely by Jumbie. For the next
twenty minutes they pranced, danced, and sang half naked
in the pouring rain, chasing Jumbie in circles. They would
stop to count the seconds after each flash, and stood with
arms outstretched, eyes closed and faces skywards, waiting
to feel their world shake around them. Exhausted, they finally fell to the ground. Peter looked up and caught a glimpse
of Granny standing on the veranda leaning on her broom,
shaking her head.

CHAPTER 24

THE BELL RANG, a prayer recital, and the students quickly left the school grounds. The lunch routine was a shortcut through the Catholic cemetery to meet Ivan and his mother at the nearby tennis club. Lunch consisted of sandwiches and drinks mixed with sporadic conversation, a quick game of table tennis and then a scramble back to school. The club was nicknamed "the white people's club" since the only members appeared to be the few whites now living on the island. It was empty at midday except for the Anglican minister who used it as a safe haven for having several bottles of Guinness Ale.

Peter missed his ride home after school, which meant riding his bike through three villages and a rainstorm before getting to the small village at the bottom of the hill where he left his bike and trudged up to the house. He quickly got undressed, wrapped a towel around him, grabbed a kettle of hot water from the wood stove in the kitchen and ran to the bathhouse. He poured the hot water into the large basin and scooped water from the large tub of rainwater until it was warm, then sat in the basin and splashed himself with closed eyes. It was one of his favorite times of the day, but he knew today he couldn't linger, and quickly stepped back out, dumped the dirty water onto the concrete floor to drain outside, and ran upstairs to dress just in time for the familiar sound of the dinner bell.

At the table there was a formality where good manners

were expected, and the boys kept silent unless asked a question, while kicking each other under the table. Hazel carved the chicken while Evelyn carried the side dishes around the table, making grotesque signs with her mouth when only the boys were looking.

It was another weekend visit with Granny, and Peter walked into the music room for his lesson, and when it was over, she pulled out a wrinkled photograph.

"Here he is. Grandpa Ivan." Peter looked down at the faded image of a thin man with dark hair, a mustache and scruffy beard. The beady eyes had a penetrating look and his face was harsh. He stared at the picture.

"So this is the famous Ivan Narodny?"

"That's not his real name. It was really Jaan Sibul. He had to change it when he came to America," she said. "In fact, he had other names before, but he kept the Ivan Narodny."

"Why did he keep changing his name?"

"When he escaped from prison, he had to change his identity to protect himself." She looked at Peter who was riveted by every word.

"You said there were many prisoners in jail, and most of them died. So how did Grandpa stay alive?"

She reached over and pushed his unkempt hair away from his eyes. "When you spend that much time in isolation, you have plenty of time to think. Your grandfather had a dream, and not the kind you have when you sleep. This is the kind of dream that never goes away and no one can take from you. It becomes your reason for living. Your grandfather survived because he had such a dream."

"Really? A dream?"

"Yes. If you look at everything great that has ever been

accomplished in the world, it came from someone with a dream. Everything starts with just a thought, and when that thought turns into a powerful dream, nothing can stop it."

"And what was Grandpa's dream?"

"In the beginning, it was freedom for his people, and when he was in prison, it became freedom for himself, a dream of escape. He knew he could never be free in Russia so he dreamt of freedom in another country. When he escaped to America, he renewed his dream of a freedom for Russia, and he knew it would take a revolution to get there. With the help of many people, that revolution took place and Russia became free from the rule of the Czar. His dream finally came true."

Peter stared in awe. "That's incredible. Thanks Granny."

You're welcome. I hope you have such a dream some day."

She patted his shoulder and left the room. He sat staring at her back as she walked out the door.

Twenty minutes later he was standing at the base of the boisflow tree looking up into the branches with Ivan next to him. "You can't be serious about this. It will take forever to cut this tree down with a cutlass, so what the hell do you think you're doing?"

"I want to build a raft, okay?" Ivan said as he took off his shirt. "Come on, let's do it!"

"A raft? Are you crazy?" Peter said, watching him swing the sharp cutlass at the trunk, sending chips flying. "Tell me something crazy man, when we cut this tree down and build this ship of yours, where do you plan on launching it?"

"In the pool."

"You mean the water tank? Are you nuts? That is the same size as any raft you could build!"

"So what? Lets build one anyway!" More chips flew out as

he kept swinging his cutlass.

"And how the hell are we going to get the logs up the hill back to the house to build this ship?"

Ivan kept chopping at the tree as he spoke, "I brought some rope to drag them back. Now come on, start cutting!"

Reluctantly, Peter picked up his cutlass and started chopping the other side of the trunk.

An hour later the tree came crashing down, missing Peter by inches. It was another hour before they had three logs cut and tied together, and Ivan slipped the cutlasses into the rope securing them.

"Okay, I'll pick it up and push and you pull the rope in front." Ivan said.

The logs were heavy and cumbersome and Peter pulled on the rope as Ivan put both legs over them and lifted with each pull.

"You know what? This is bullshit!" Peter said.

"We're almost there,"

"We're not even half way!"

Ivan bent over and lifted the logs over a fallen branch. Peter grabbed the rope and pulled hard.

He heard the scream and turned back and saw Ivan crumble. His face was white as paper and his mouth wide open. Peter looked at what he was grabbing and saw blood gushing between his fingers, coming from the back of his leg. Ivan took his hand away and looked down at a six-inch slash, exposing the bone. His toes had flipped forward and were resting against his shin and his foot appeared to be severed. Peter looked at the open blade of the cutlass tied to logs, and stood speechless, his hand at his mouth. The blood was pumping over Ivan's legs and hands and they were both momentarily paralyzed, staring at the river of red.

"OH MY GOD! OH MY GOD!" Ivan was gasping for breath and tried to cover the wound. "HELP!"

Peter looked down helplessly. "HERE! TIE THIS AROUND IT!" He shouted, and helped wrap the rope above the cut to stop the bleeding. The gushing subsided and now came in spurts.

"OH MY GOD, I AM GOING TO DIE."

"JESUS CHRIST! WHAT CAN I DO?" Peter screamed "SHIT! I CAN'T CARRY YOU! WHAT CAN I DO?"

"CHRISTIAN!" Ivan screamed, "RUN AND GET CHRISTIAN!"

"OK. Keep that tourniquet going! I'll get him." Peter touched Ivan's shoulder as tears streamed down his face. He turned and ran through the bush with Jumbie at his heels. It was a long way back up the hill and he ran up to the clearing below the house to catch his breath. He tried to scream for Christian but no sound came out. He sat on the ground panting and suddenly something made him stop and listen. Then he heard it, the distant sound of Christian whistling. He found him naked, taking a bath under a tree by splashing water over his body from a drum. Christian took one look at his face and knew something terrible had happened.

"CHRISTIAN! COME QUICK! IVAN CUT HIMSELF IN THE BUSH! QUICK!"

Christian quickly pulled his pants on and ran over to him. "Where is he?"

"Down there!" Peter pointed. "By the Boisflow tree! Quick! Help him!"

As if guided by something supernatural, the giant, half-naked man leaped over the tall grass and down the hill, disappearing into the forest with Jumbie showing him the way. Peter collapsed on the ground and cried but suddenly realized that

Ivan would have to get to the hospital and he ran to the house. He found Viola on the back veranda sitting on a wooden box, reading the bible. She didn't need anything but his face and evidence of blood to know how bad it was, and she ran to the phone to help him make the call. She grabbed the phone and cranked the handle, and prayed while it rang. The operator said she would try and get through to Mary and five long rings later Mary answered. After a stunned silence, she said she would be up as quickly as possible. Viola called the hospital but the only ambulance was in the garage for repairs. When she put the phone back on its cradle Peter looked at her and buried his face into her shoulder.

Christian arrived moments later with Ivan in his arms, both were covered with blood. He was unconscious when he laid him in the bed.

"Is he dead?" Peter asked.

"No, not yet, but he needs to get to de hospital quick." It was the first time Peter had ever detected fear in Christian's voice.

"My mother is coming. We called her."

"Thank the Lord for that" Christian said. "Quick! Give me de sheet off your bed."

Peter ripped the sheet off and Christian tore it into strips, and quickly wrapped it around the wound. The makeshift bandage quickly turned red as Peter held the rope tourniquet, loosening it when he saw the leg turn blue.

Granny walked in to see what the commotion was all about. At the sight of Ivan on the bed covered in blood, the tears in Peter's eyes, and Viola on her knees praying, she muttered something in Russian, and leaned on the table for support. She kept shaking her head, and quickly left the room.

Peter watched the surreal scene before him. He listened

to the sobbing, and the voice of Viola begging God to spare Ivan's life, and stillness came over him. He felt as if he was being lifted up and watching the scene from above. He saw the large dark figure leaning over a lean white body, a kneeling woman with a head wrapped in cloth holding the boy's hand, and a black dog watching from the corner. He was re-living the scene when he looked down on his own body in the same room after drinking the kerosene.

Forty minutes later the sound of a car came through the window and Christian gently lifted Ivan off the bed and carried him outside. Mary was visibly shaken when she saw the sheet-white face, the sea of blood, and her unconscious son. She steadied herself on Christian's shoulder as he lay him in the back seat. She looked back at Peter, whose mouth was still open in shock. "I'll get him to the hospital. Stay here with Granny," she said in a trembling voice. She jumped behind the wheel, slammed the door and the car skidded around the corner.

Later that evening the phone line was dead and Peter thought about how it had worked earlier, and remembered the words of his teacher about believing in miracles.

The next day he told Brother Gorman what happened. "I will call the hospital," he said.

Moments later he called Peter out of class "He is okay. He cut his foot to the bone and severed the Achilles tendon. They said that if he had lost any more blood he wouldn't have made it. They operated on him for three hours and he is now under sedation. It is a miracle that he is alive because there were three doctors who are nuns who happened to be visiting the island, and were at the hospital when he was brought in. When they saw his condition and no one there to help, they volunteered to work on him." He looked down at Peter whose eyes were wide open. "Tell me, how did this happen?"

Peter relayed the story of the raft building and cutting down the tree, and the Brother's face was solemn. "The Lord has spared his live and is sending you a message." Peter looked at him and said nothing. "You need to understand that there are no accidents in this world. Everything happens for a reason. It was not his time. It could have easily been you but it is the same message. If that voice inside you says that something is not right, then don't do it. Do you understand?"

"Yes, Brother. But what is that voice you speak of?"

"That's God talking to you. If you want to know if something is right, just ask Him and He will answer. Some call it intuition but it is God who is guiding you. Remember that. Now I want you to take the afternoon off and go see your brother."

"Thank you." Peter ran outside to his bicycle. He pedaled quickly to the other side of town and up the hill to the hospital, thinking about the voice within him and how many times it had spoken to him and he just didn't listen.

The nurse pointed to the door and he opened it slowly. Mary was sitting on a chair next to the bed and looked up. Ivan lay on his back with eyes closed, and very pale. His right leg was thickly bandaged up to the knee. Mary motioned for him to go back outside and she followed him, closing the door gently, and a nun dressed in white walked towards them. Her face was small and she wore round glasses, and was holding a rosary in one hand.

"How's he doing?" she asked.

"He's still asleep. Are you the one who operated on him?" Mary asked.

"Yes, and fortunately, I happen to specialize in reconstructive surgery, but I must tell you that given the facilities here, this was one of the most challenging operations I have ever done." She paused and looked at Peter in his school uniform and looked back at Mary.

"He cut every muscle and nerve in his leg. It took eighty-five stitches and he lost a tremendous amount of blood. If you didn't have the same blood type, he would not have made it since they have no blood stored here. This place is as bad as a hospital I visited in Africa. Do you know they didn't have enough bandages? They actually washed some to use again while we waited. Then the lights went off and I had to finish the operation by kerosene lamps. Incredible! Anyway, I'm glad to have done God's work. I am leaving the island tomorrow and I just wanted to see how he was doing before I left."

"Will he be able to walk again?" Mary asked.

"I don't know for sure. He will have to stay on his back for several weeks and then use crutches -- if you can find some. The rest is up to the good Lord."

"Thank you so much," Mary said and they shook hands. Peter watched as the nun walked briskly down the barren hall.

CHAPTER 25

PETER WENT UP alone to visit Granny and gave a silent groan when the car turned into the Batwoman's driveway. Without a word, Mr. Ford got out and Peter leaned back, closed his eyes, and listened to the ubiquitous sound of the crickets.

When he finally emerged, Peter looked over and sniffed twice, curious about the strange odor that overpowered the usual rum and beer. They drove in silence. When he got to the house, he ran into his bedroom and found Jumbie waiting on his bed. The next morning he told Granny of Ivan's condition and she listened in silence.

"I'm going to tell Christian," he said, and ran out the door.

"That's great news, mon." Christain said with a smile.

"You saved his life."

"I am glad I was here, that's for sure," Christian said, smiling. "You boys are like family to me." There was a moment of silence as they stared at each other, and Peter slowly nodded his head. "Hey, come for dinner tonight, I go cook for you, all right? I have something special."

"Okay, I'll be there." Peter turned and walked back to the house.

He hurried through breakfast and went into the piano room where Granny was waiting.

"I am so happy he is okay," she said, as soon as he settled next to her. "Let me ask you, why do you boys do such crazy things? Build a raft? Where were you going to use it?"

"In the water tank on the hill" he replied.

"Peter, I have seen that tank, and it is too small to float anything! I don't understand."

"I don't know, Granny. I thought it was crazy but it was just something to do."

"Well, right now let's make some music." She opened *Piano Adventures* and pointed to the page.

The time went by quickly. Maria explained the relationships between the different notes as she struck the keys and asked him to do the same.

"Do you know what makes the music?" she asked.

Peter looked at her, not quite sure what to say. "Is it the sound you make when you hit the keys?"

"Not exactly. Listen." She struck a note, and then hit another, and another. She did that with many notes, waiting a few seconds between them. "Would you call that music?"

"Not really," Peter said.

"Now listen." She raised both hands off the keys and came down on them slowly. For the next minute she played a beautiful piece that left him mesmerized. "Now, would you call that music?"

"Yes, of course."

"So what is the difference?"

"I give up. Is it the time you took between playing the notes?"

"Exactly! Music is created by the space between the notes, not by the notes themselves. A note by itself is just a sound. Does that make sense?"

"Yes, it does."

"This is true of life itself. The music of life is the time we take between the notes we hit all day. You can pound away at random, but it is important to stop and think. Let your mind rest. Close your eyes and sit quietly once in a while. The music will come to you." She looked at Peter who was staring at her. "Can you do that for me?"

"I'll try," He said.

"That is something your grandfather taught me. He said that is the time when things become clear, when your purpose in life becomes obvious. Some call it meditation. He perfected this practice in prison when all he had to live for existed only in his mind. He said great thoughts would come to you if you just rest the mind for a moment, and pay attention to the images. You need to do this for yourself."

"Yes, Granny."

She smiled at him, got up slowly, and left the room.

That afternoon Jumbie was waiting for him at the top of the marble steps, and together they walked into the woods to the bamboo grove, his favorite hiding place since infancy. He sat and listened to the wind make music as it swept through the tall bamboo. He thought about what his grandmother had said as the wind changed speeds, making different notes, creating symphonies of its own. He sat for an hour, absorbing his new appreciation for the grove and its music until Jumbie licked his leg, telling him it was time to go. He got up and walked out as the sun sank behind the mountain, and headed towards Christian's house to have the promised meal.

Christian still lived in the tiny shack with a rusted galvanize roof and a wooden floor which sagged when walked on. A wood partition separated his small bed from the rest of the house where he kept a bench and gardening tools. He was cooking in the back yard and looked up and grinned. He reached in his pocket and handed Peter a letter. "Hey mon, please read dis for me. I get it last week from my son. It's the first letter I ever get from him."

Christian could not read very well, and he liked it when the boys visited him so he could have the newspaper or a story read to him. Peter walked over and sat down on a log followed closely by Christian who sat across from him. He looked at the envelope and noticed the stamps were from England, tore open the envelope, and looked at the one page letter. The penmanship was flawless, and the words were bold and clear. He read it without stopping. When he finished and read "your faithful son, Damen," his eyes moved up to Christian who was staring at him, absorbing every word, and he saw a lonely tear trickle down his cheek. In the fading light it looked like melting wax, and his large bare chest heaved as he caught his breath. Peter was surprised that his hero was even capable of crying, but now, hearing the words from his son, he let the tears flow. The two of them sat on fallen tree trunks while the radiance of the setting sun cast dancing shadows all around them. These were tears of joy, which came when he heard that his boy was now settled in England, going to school during the day and working at night as a janitor. It was a dream come true for Christian who had saved for years from working on the estate, and wanted nothing more than to give his son the opportunity that he never had himself.

After a few moments Peter asked, "Are you all right?"

"Yeah mon, I'm okay." Christian wiped his face with his massive hands. He wore no shirt and his muscular body was sweating from the heat, now dissipating as the night descended upon them. He reached behind him and handed Peter strips of fresh sugar cane. He bit into one and felt the sweet juice sink into his mouth and watched Christian as he threw more wood on the fire where the meal was cooking. Sparks flew up when he uncovered the large pot, stirred and tasted its contents, and nodded in approval.

"You hungry? I have a good meal for supper."

"You always make a good 'braf', so what's on de menu?"

"You know what? Dis time you can't ask, just eat, all right?"

"No problem, I'm sure it's good."

They talked and joked while Christian tended the fire and kept stirring, tasting, and adding spices. The pot emitted a wonderful aroma as he filled a small wooden bowl with some meat, boiled plantains and vegetables, and handed it to Peter.

"Try dis, I think you will like it," he said smiling.

They ate and talked, and Peter relished what he had been served. He looked up and Christian was staring at him.

"Hey, you know what you eating?" He was looking at him sideways. There was something about his look that made Peter hesitate.

"Rabbit. Dis here is rabbit and it damn good too!"

His shiny teeth broke through his thick lips. "Sorry, but dis time you wrong."

"Not rabbit? Den what is it?"

"I can't tell you dat."

"What de hell you mean, you can't tell me?"

"If I tell you, I don't want you to be vexed with me, okay?" Christian spoke quickly.

"Now why would I get vexed with you?"

"Okay, I tell you but make sure you don't get vexed, okay?"

"No problem," Peter said and stared at him.

"What you eating dere is cat."

"CAT? Christian, what you mean cat, where de hell you get cat from?" Peter's shock came as no surprise to the old West Indian who looked at him calmly. There was a silence and Peter saw Christian's eyes blaze in the light from the fire.

He spoke slowly. "That's your cat." He said, and looked

away quickly.

Peter sat in stunned silence with his fork in mid-air, holding what turned out to be a piece of his pet at the end of it.

"WHAT? MY CAT? TELL ME YOU JOKING! MY CAT? SUNSHINE?"

Christian kept poking at the fire. "I not making joke. Look, de cat was getting old and when a cat get old it run back into de bush to die, so I just get it before it leave. I mean, why waste good meat like dat?"

Peter's mouth was still open as he stared at him in disbelief.

Christian continued talking. "Where you think a man like myself could get meat from? I only have one cow for milk, two chickens for eggs, one rabbit which I saving for Christmas, and my dog, and I don't eat dog." There was a moment of silence. "I sorry, mon, but I really doing you and de cat a big favor,"

Peter looked down at his fork which was still holding a piece of Sunshine, listening to the rationale of why his friend should have killed and eaten his cat, and then served it to him, because it was the right thing to do.

"Christian, what de hell makes you think the cat was running away?"

"I time it. Listen, from de time you get de cat I give it three years before it go back to de bush, de natural place of origin. I get de timing from de first cat you get."

"Christian, I got my first cat when I was about one year old and have had maybe ten cats since."

"I know dat."

The implication of his answer sank in. "NO! CHRISTIAN! DON'T TELL ME! ALL THE REST OF THEM? YOU DIDN'T!"

"Yeah mon." The impish grin reappeared.

"All these years, Christian, you've been eating our cats?" Peter looked at him in horror.

Christian stopped poking the fire and looked at him, smoke wafting across his rugged face as he rubbed his broad nose with the back of his hand. He smiled broadly, and resumed his nervous fire poking.

"So when our cats disappeared, they never ran away. You just ate them, is that right?"

"Dat's right," he said.

"Christian...." He stopped short, at a loss of words and just stared at him. There was silence except for the intermittent popping of burning wood, and Peter looked up at the fireflies flickering in the trees above him as they blended in with the rising sparks. He looked down at the half empty bowl, stirred it, and very cautiously, he continued eating, chewing slowly. Christian looked at him warily and their eyes met, staring at each other for a long time. Peter looked back at his bowl, trying to digest the horror of what he had done, and at Christian's face, that now depicted some fear. He kept shaking his head and began to chuckle. His shoulders started to shake and it wasn't long before he dropped his fork and doubled over, laughing loudly, and Jumbie began to bark. Christian went over to him, came down to his knees and put his big hand on his shoulder and their foreheads touched as they caught glimpses of each other through warm tears of joy. The filtered moonlight portrayed his black-pitted face against Peter's smooth white skin, and the darkness enveloped them and the Royal Palms waved from a distance, as the wild things around them relished their happiness and drank their mirth.

CHAPTER 26

IVAN WAS LIKE a caged animal at the hospital, unable to walk and confined to bed. When Mary took him home, he hobbled around on crude crutches and fell, ripping the stitches, and his fear of never walking again intensified. The wide, six-inch horseshoe scar at the back of his leg was a frightening sight.

Without a playmate, Peter sought new distractions and joined the school's cricket team where he found himself quickly outclassed by the rest of the boys that had been playing in the streets since infancy. He had doubts about the sport and watched the island's team play the neighboring islands in a "Test Match" which went on for days, with runs scored in the hundreds. It was a spectacle that made no sense to him, and his cricket career came to a quick end.

When Ivan was finally back on his feet, a new and exciting source of entertainment came into their lives. Angus and Neville, brothers who lived in the center of town, were friends from school. Their parents, a red-haired Irish woman and a local father, treated Ivan and Peter as family and provided a safe haven for them. A close friendship blossomed and the lure of the ocean became a common passion.

The idea of sailing sparked Angus to take up the challenge of building a boat. Well aware of their last raft-building attempt, he sought little advice from the brothers and relied on some plans in *Popular Mechanics,* and began construction in the attic of their home. The boat was to be an eight-foot "pram" - a small snub-nosed sailboat with a flat bottom, and the project took planning and collecting materials. Angus appeared to have a natural talent and went at it with an earnest determination that caught everyone's attention.

Three months later all the boys crowded into the small attic to admire the finished craft. Suddenly, Ivan looked at the boat, then at the only small door into the room. "Hey, Angus," he shouted. "I have a question. How do you plan on getting this vessel out of here?"

Everyone looked at the boat and the door. Angus reached down and picked up a tape measure and quickly measured the height and width of the boat and did the same to the door.

"Shit!" he said. "Shit! Shit! Shit!" While the others looked on, he walked over and measured the window, throwing open both shutters. "Hey, it just fits!" he proclaimed.

"That's great, except we are three floors up from the street," Ivan said. "What do you suggest, you push it out, and we all go down and catch it?"

More silence and disturbed looks were exchanged, broken up with a cough and a guffaw. "Screw you guys," Angus said. "We'll get it out the window and lower it down to the street. Tomorrow, when the paint is dry, I want everyone to come back and help, okay? I'll get the rope." He spoke with authority.

"Yeah mon, we'll be here. We wouldn't want to miss this," said Peter. Neville stood next to him, trying hard not to laugh.

The next day the four boys congregated in the small room. Everyone had an opinion on the best way to get the boat out of the room and down to the street, and after much heated conversation, they tied a rope through the mast hole and carefully pushed the boat sideways out the window. Angus' shouts about scratching the paint went unheeded, and with everyone holding on to the rope, the craft was lowered to the street below where by now, a small crowd had collected and traffic had come to a halt. Half way down, the boat was tied off on while the three boys raced downstairs and waited while Angus inched the boat down to their waiting hands. Everyone applauded when it touched the ground and Angus was beaming.

"Just as I planned!" he said.

"That's bullshit, but let's go sailing!" Ivan shouted .

More excited conversation ensued and everyone volunteered to help carry the craft to the bay-front just a block away. They gently lay it on the rocky shore, and after more banter and back slapping, walked back to the house.

It took several more days to get the boat rigged and ready for its maiden voyage. Now the four friends stood and admired the white hull, red sails and varnished mast.

"What are we going to name it?" Neville asked.

"Barnacle," Angus said quickly. "I want to call it Barnacle."

"Barnacle? What the hell for?" Everyone laughed except Angus.

"Okay, you built it, you can call it what you want," Neville said as he pulled out a small can of paint. "How do you spell Barnacle? Is it Barnicle or Barnacle?"

After another heated debate, the jury was split and the boat had a different spelling of its name on each side, and while the paint dried, Neville produced a bottle of beer for the christening.

"What? No champagne?" Angus opened his hands.

"Maybe for the next yacht you build," Neville said, as he shook the bottle and poured the beer over the bow. More laughter ensued and they picked up the boat and carried it towards the water, eager to begin their sailing careers. Angus raised the patchy red sail, recently stained and not quite dry, pushed off into the calm sea while his friends clapped and screamed advice from the shore.

Barnacle was only large enough for two bodies at a time, so the group paired up and took turns going out, raising the sails, managing the tiller, and catching the sporadic gusts of wind that swept down from the valley above. Everyone wanted to be captain and yet amidst the screams, laughter, and cursing, they were all able to maneuver the boat safely around the harbor. It was a joyous afternoon, the birth of a new pastime, and endless hours of happiness for the four friends.

CHAPTER **27**

THE BOYS BEGGED their mother to let them stay in town for Carnival, and she reluctantly agreed. The day before it began, Mary left them with a large family in town with strict instructions on expected behavior, all of which fell on deaf ears. The boys had dreamt about Carnival since infancy. Their school friends had always talked about nothing else for months before, and when the town took on the captivating mood of celebration before the festival, they felt deprived by retreating to the country. Now their teenage years brought on a passion for discovery, and a desire to mix with the crowd, especially the opposite sex. Mary showed little enthusiasm for having them subjected to the famous bacchanal, and had avoided it as long as she could. Peter once overheard her describe it as " An excuse to commit those sins you've always wanted to." He wasn't quite sure what that meant, but was curious to find out, because he knew what a sin was. Now she realized that it was time for some exposure.

It was Friday evening when they walked through the narrow streets and became quickly engulfed by the steel-band music. They moved out to the main road and were met by throngs of people dancing, laughing and drinking. A full moon hung listlessly over the town, lighting the path for the revelers that all walked in unison with a sway and a dance, filling the air with laughter and sound. A steel-band was gathering at the corner in obvious disorganization and friendly disagreement, and Calypso singers were on the opposite corner in a small circle, composing songs about anything scandalous or political.

Peter walked over to the group of singers who made room for him. Snapping their fingers, hitting a tin can for the beat, and moving their bodies in rhythm, they took turns humming and making up verses, and Peter joined the circle. A thickset man handed him a small cup of rum. He took a swig, and tried to hide the grimace as he listened to the budding Calypsonian hold up his hands for everyone to listen:

"Carnival time is here at last
De time for us to play de mas
And look at changes all around
Even de white boy come to town
So let us show him how to fete in style
And find a woman who go make him smile."

Everyone laughed, and Peter felt his back slapped as another bottle of rum was passed around, and the songs continued about the weather, girlfriends, wives, and politics. Peter wallowed in the mood and watched a rum bottle coming his way. He took a swig and his eyes opened wide.

"What was that?" he gasped.

"White rum. Have another one," the singer said.

"Jesus! Dat stuff is poison!"

His face turned red, and he coughed and spat into the gutter. His head was spinning as he backed away from the laughing crowd and moved slowly down the road. He absorbed the sights, sounds and smells of the town and felt an exuberance he had never felt before as he weaved his way back to his room.

The excitement intensified the next day with a steelband and calypso competition in the park. The rivalry between the bands was passionate, with groups of fifty men pounding at the oil drums that had been cut and tuned to produce different notes and sounds. The ground seemed to move to the rhythm while everyone danced, with arms flailing and bottoms shaking. The hypnotic scene mesmerized Peter and the gleam never left his face. The time went by quickly and he had trouble avoiding the continuous appearance of a rum bottle or cold beer. Knowing he had a couple long days ahead of him, he made his way back to his room by sunset and found Ivan already lying inert in the bed next to him.

Sunday came quickly and Peter woke up late with the novel experience of a blistering hangover. He lay in bed, swearing to himself that he would never again have rum pass his lips. He heard the distant clanging of the church bells, reminding everyone that carnival or not, it was still the day of worship, and he wondered how many of the faithful would show up in church, after the way he saw some behave the day before. This was the day before the street "jump-up" and the streets were soon full of eager faces, festive clothing, and the ubiquitous rum bottle. As he merged with the crowds, he heard the never-ending sounds of steel drums and smelled the frying fish and Johnny Cakes being sold on the sidewalks.

When night descended on the town, the mood changed, and everyone prepared for the traditional "Papishow." This was the "warm-up" for the next two days and for this night only, "cross-dressing" was accepted, and everyone made attempts, albeit weak ones, to look like the opposite sex. This practice brought much amusement as the crowds took to the streets and Peter quickly jumped in with a line of merrymakers and sweating bodies. He heard his name called out and looked up to the veranda where he recognized people who were pointing and laughing at him. He was an easy target - the lone white face in a sea of brown and black, with his arms draped over a beautiful dark-skinned girl who was wearing a seductive smile that had sent his innocent heart throbbing. As they moved in unison through the streets and into the night, the thought occurred to him that, with some of the men dressed up as women, that his new love may not be exactly what she appeared to be. He kept staring at her and after several more beers, his mind began to wonder. In his naïve innocence, and just to be certain, he reached across and squeezed her right breast and was quickly gratified to find out that it was real. With no obvious desire to know his intent, and embarrassed by the public display, the beauty queen grabbed his arm from off her shoulder, took his face in one hand and turned it towards her. With the speed of a boxer, she slapped him hard across the face, turned, and quickly disappeared into the crowd. Peter stood there, stunned and heartbroken, as the throng moved around him with amused looks on their faces. He waited until everyone had gone past and with embarrassment and a stinging face, he walked quickly back to his room, having just had his first experience of rejection by the opposite sex.

All was forgotten when he awoke next morning to the sound of music blown in by the warm breeze. He rushed through breakfast and chatted excitedly with Ivan. They made a quick exit and walked to Angus' house where they would get a front row seat to the day's events from the veranda above the main street of town. It was already packed with a raucous crowd, and Peter watched as the streets filled up with an ocean of bobbing heads and wild costumes. Everyone was in a wonderful mood and the rum, beer and whiskey started to flow. Now the sound of a steel-band coming down the street filled the air and it was soon directly below him, pounding out their music and followed by several hundred people, dancing and gyrating with looks of ecstasy on their faces. The house shook with the pulsating beat of the music, and Peter was mesmerized by the magic of the moment. He felt a warm hand around his neck and turned to the soft eyes of a beautiful brown-skinned girl standing next to him. She placed her other hand on her hip, tilted her head and said, "I can't stand here no more. Let's go!" She grabbed his hand and they ran down the stairs and quickly became one with the sea of gyrating bodies. They sang and danced until the sweat poured off their bodies. Rum was passed around which Peter swallowed, despite the lingering memory of the day before. He held on tightly to the girl's bare shoulders, careful not to touch her bobbing breasts, which by sight alone, he was not about to authenticate.

"What's your name?" he shouted in her ear, catching a whiff of the gardenia perfume mixed in with the sweet odor of her perspiring body.

She grabbed the back of his neck and pulled him close. "Rosemarie!" she said, giving his earlobe a nibble. The sound of the pounding drums seemed to get louder and they continued shuffling down the street before he leaned over and said, "My name is Peter".

She looked back at him, pulled him close again and shouted gently "I know that!"

He squeezed her shoulder and closed his eyes. They moved in unison down the street as one, and Peter kept thinking that this had to be the heaven the Brothers had talked about.

The music and dancing never seemed to end as the day drifted by, and the heat and humidity increased, along with the consumption of alcohol. Articles of clothing seemed to be falling off the sweating bodies of the beautiful women that surrounded him, and Peter stared in fascination. Rosemarie pinched him hard when he had trouble taking his eyes off a woman who seemed to have lost her top. He looked up and saw people pointing at him from the verandas above, waving and laughing. He recognized some, others knew who he was, and for the rest of them, he was a Carnival novelty. He had a quick thought that his mother was going to get an earful that he would have to explain, but for the moment, he didn't care. He felt safe and content in the flood, dancing to the pulsating rhythm of steel drums with one of the most beautiful girls he had ever met, and he wished the exhilaration would never end.

It was well after midnight before the bands started to disperse and he became acutely aware of his hunger, fatigue and throbbing head. Exhausted packs of revelers were shuffling down the street, moving their feet in unison singing:

"Anou allez ah kai mama nous!

Come go home, anou allez!"

"Let's go home to our mother's house." As Peter watched some of the couples, he knew for sure not everyone was going to end up at their own house if they ended up in a house at all. Depleted and content, he wondered what would happen next when Rosemarie took his hand and squeezed it. She led him to several streets away, opened a side gate and pulled him to the side of the two-story house.

"Too bad, my mother is home," she whispered, with her arm over his shoulder as she pulled him close to her.

He leaned over and kissed her and they held each other tightly. He felt the warmth of her body and some novel sensations came over him, and she giggled. A dog started barking from the upstairs veranda.

"Rosemarie? Is that you?" A woman's voice came through the window.

"Yes, mama, it's me," she said, and Peter could feel her hot breath against his cheek.

"Who is that with you? Come upstairs now."

"You better go," she whispered and she kissed him again, holding him tightly.

"Okay. See you tomorrow?" he asked.

"Don't come here. Mama will be here."

"Okay," he said and he reached over and gave her another kiss, then went quickly out the gate when he heard someone coming down the stairs.

He walked briskly through the streets back to the house. He entered through the back door and passed the table with leftover food. He stuffed cold chicken and mashed potatoes into his mouth, washing it down with half a bottle of warm beer. He chewed vigorously while he made his way up to his room and collapsed onto his side of the large bed. Through half-shut eyes, he saw the heap of his brother next to him from which emanated loud, distorted snores. He turned on his back and watched dizzy visions on the dark ceiling above him, broken up by light patterns from the passing cars. He sighed deeply, touched his lips and smiled, and was soon lost in pleasant hallucinations.

It poured rain the next morning on the last day of carnival, and Peter roamed the streets in search of his Rosemarie. The damp mood changed when the sky cleared and music filled the air, and crowds poured back onto the streets. His eyes scanned the faces, and he felt dumb not having arranged a meeting place with her, but finally gave up and joined the merrymakers until nightfall. Wet and exhausted, he retired early and lay in bed, full of dizzy images of his lost love.

CHAPTER **28**

MARY HAD SPORADIC communication with her parents back in Massachusetts, and this time the letter was a plea for help. A month later a check arrived with the note "Here is what's left of your inheritance," and Mary felt a deep sense of relief. The money would provide a small nest egg for her future and hopefully get the boys off the island. Ivan would be the first to go, and applications were sent to boarding schools in the U.S. but the first rejection letter came back quickly, claiming "a lack of proper test results," and "We believe that the applicant could not adapt to life at a private school in America." Now the boys began to realize the probability of spending the rest of their lives on the island, and their dreams of escape intensified.

The arrival of an acceptance letter from a small school in upstate New York created tremendous excitement. Darrow was a boarding school in an old converted Shaker village in New Lebanon, a remote town famous for its severe winters.

As Ivan's departure date approached, the boys went up to say farewell to Granny. She took their hands and Peter felt the trembling of her thin fingers, and a sense of sadness came over him, realizing how frail she had become. It rained heavily all weekend so the boys played poker and found old comics of *Flash Gordon, the Lone Ranger, and Batman*, and devoured their childhood fantasies.

Mary was sick when Ivan was scheduled to leave, so

Peter went with him to the airport with Seamon the taxi driver. At the terminal, Ivan went to check his bags and Peter looked over at the counter and was stunned when he recognized Rosemarie.

He walked over and her mouth fell open.

"Well, look who it is, my island boy himself."

"Where have you been?" Peter asked, and his eyes flickered in disbelief.

"Where have I been? I've been here waiting for you!"

"I didn't know you worked here, besides you're a long way from where I left you."

"I told you at carnival where I worked, but I think you had your mind elsewhere."

The sound of the approaching plane distracted him. "I'll come back to see you," Peter whispered as he walked away.

"You do that. I'll be here waiting."

The plane approached over the distant mountain and then suddenly turned, dipping low over a field of coconut trees, one wing skimming their tops. It dropped quickly at the far end of the runway and the wheels threw out dark smoke and the nose lurched forward, braking sharply. It finally came to a halt within a few feet of the end of the short runway and the crashing Atlantic surf.

Ivan walked towards the plane and up the steps, looked back and waved, then disappeared into the tired looking aircraft. It taxied towards the mountainside, turned, and with full throttle, sped towards the ocean, lifting off just before the end of the runway.

As Peter watched it vanish into the low clouds, he felt sadness and a sense of loss. He walked back in and saw Rosemarie talking on the phone, with a line of people in front of her. He got her attention, waved, and sent her a kiss. She returned it, motioning for him to call her. Outside, Seamon was waiting for the white couple that had gotten off the plane. "Taxi?" he shouted.

"Yes, please." The woman shouted.

The man walked towards them and Seamon picked up their suitcases and put them in the trunk.

Peter got in next to Seamon and the two visitors climbed in the back. They were both wearing wool clothing and sweating profusely.

"My God, that plane ride was scary!" the woman said. Her face was pasty white, and she quickly stripped off her sweater.

"Can you take us to town?" the man asked. He was small in stature, wore thick glasses, and had a pasty complexion.

"Yes, sir, I can do that," said Seamon

"Great! How far is it?" he asked.

"Not too far."

"I see, and how long does it take to get there?" the man asked.

"Not too long" said Seamon as he started the car with a loud backfire, which caused the woman to jump in her seat and quickly roll down her window.

"Ummm. Okay, then how much does it cost?"

"Not too much," was the quick reply at which the couple looked at each other and their wide eyes displayed increased anxiety. The man looked at Seamon who had turned to back the car out of his parking place.

"God damn it, man! Give me a straight answer! How much will it cost me!"

Seamon looked over at Peter and back at his passenger. "Twenty-five dollars, sir. The trip is about an hour and a half unless we stop somewhere, all right?"

"Thank you, that's what I wanted to know and I don't want

to stop anywhere." He pushed his glasses up the bridge of his red nose and rolled down his window.

Seamon put the car in gear and it lurched forward and crossed the narrow bridge over the first of many rivers. They rode in silence along the coast and through the first village. Peter glanced back occasionally and saw the couple gazing at the passing scenes of a rugged coastline and unhurried villagers.

"Where are you from?" Peter turned and asked the couple, attempting to break the silence.

"Canada" said the man without hesitation.

"What brings you to this island?"

"I'm an efficiency expert and the government has asked that I visit to make some recommendations, especially in the hospital."

Peter and Seamon looked at each other and quickly looked away to prevent a fit of laughter. Without turning around he said, "That's great. Welcome to Dominica. You certainly have your work cut out for you."

"Umm, aren't you visiting as well?" the man asked. Peter suddenly realized that they had thought of him as another tourist.

"No, actually I live here," he said.

"I'm sorry, but when we read about the island it said there were hardly any white residents."

"Well, you're looking at one," Seamon said, as he slowed to shift into a lower gear. They rode on in silence.

It was now dusk and he turned on the lights and moved quickly over the dark and curvy road. Peter and Seamon chatted and laughed while the couple sat staring out the window as the small Austin crossed another river and started to climb a steep hill. They turned a sharp corner and Seamon suddenly slammed on the brakes and pointed to the road in front of the car.

"Oui, Bon Dieu! Gardez Ca! Manicou!" Peter looked out and saw it. The Manicou, a nocturnal animal that resembles the agouti or possum, stood frozen in the road, caught in the bright lights as its large round eyes shone back up at them like beacons.

"Oh, my God! What is that?" the woman asked, as she looked out past them at the paralyzed creature, which was size of a small dog staring back at the car.

"That's my dinner!" said Seamon and he reached under his seat and quickly pulled out a large stick, pulled on the hand brake, and leaving the car running, quickly opened his door.

"What in God's name is going on!" shouted the man.

Peter looked back at them. "Don't worry. That's a Manicou and they make a good meal. He is going to try and get him."

"What the hell are you talking about? Are both of you crazy? Let's get out the hell out of here now!" He was clutching the back of their seat as his wife's hands were over her mouth, trying to stifle a scream.

Now Seamon was outside and slowly approaching the Manicou, which was hypnotized by the lights. He raised the stick and hit the animal on the head, throwing it back several feet into the bumper of the car. The woman screamed and the couple clutched each other, their bodies shaking.

"Oh, my God!" the woman shouted.

Peter rolled down his window and shouted, "All right, mon, you got him!"

Seamon reached down and picked up the lifeless creature by the long tail and carried it to the back of the car. As he passed the rear window the woman screamed again, seeing the creature carried upside down with blood pouring out of its long snout. Seamon opened the trunk, threw it in, and slammed it shut. He jumped back into his seat behind the wheel and looked at Peter.

"Yeah mon, I have me a good dinner now!"

"That's great, except right now you also have a problem in the back seat," Peter said, motioning to the couple behind them.

They both turned and saw the terrified bleached white faces of the couple, their arms wrapped around each other. Their mouths were open but no sound came out.

"It's okay! It's really all right! There is no danger." Peter tried to talk to them but realized it was pointless.

"Let's get the hell out of here!" the man shouted at Seamon.

"Okay. Sorry about dat. I take you to your hotel now," said Seamon and the car shot forward back up the hill.

"Please get us out of here! Hurry! How much further is it?" The man beseeched him.

"Not too far," said Seamon.

"Oh No! My God! Please help us!" The woman cried, leaning into her husband's shoulder. The two remained in the same position for the remainder of the arduous trip over the narrow mountain road and back down towards the town. Peter and Seamon had difficulty containing themselves as they realized what they had done to the innocent visitors.

"Where do you want me to drop you off?" Seamon asked Peter.

"I will spend the night at Castaways. Linda is having a little fete there tonight."

"I've heard about those fetes," he said with a grin.

Peter reached over and slapped him on the shoulder.

Soon they passed the faded Castaways sign and pulled into

the parking lot under a large mango tree and Peter opened his door. "Thanks mon, see you later," he said to Seamon, and he turned to say good night to the couple, who were now opening their doors and getting out of the car.

"Where you going? This is not your hotel," said Seamon, looking in the mirror.

"We're getting the hell out of this taxi and staying here as well." They were now both out of the car, standing next to each other in a slight drizzle, breathing heavily.

"No problem," said Peter "I'm sure Linda will have a room for you."

"Our luggage, Quickly!" The man was reaching for his wallet and pulled out some money, which he handed to Seamon, and they all walked to the back and opened the trunk. The woman reached in for her suitcase, and a terrifying screech came from inside of the trunk, and the bloodied Manicou leaped out and scrambled between the woman's legs before it scurried off into the bushes.

The woman screamed and ran back to her husband, knocking Seamon against the car. She continued screaming uncontrollably and finally collapsed to her knees on the ground.

Peter looked at Seamon, who now displayed shock and disbelief. "Jesus Christ! I thought you said the dam thing was dead!"

"I thought so, too! I must have just knocked it out!" He looked over to the man who was now on his knees next to his wife. "Sir, I am so sorry."

"Shit! I wouldn't even try that. Just give them their dam bags and get out of here!" Peter said, as he watched the small crowd of people come running out of the hotel, attracted by the commotion.

Seamon quickly carried the suitcases and put them down in front of the couple. "Holy shit, look at that!" Peter said, pointing to the bags, which were covered in blood and scratches. "You better get the hell out of here before you get killed."

Seamon turned and quickly got back into the car. He slammed it into reverse and started to back up, stopping in front of couple.

"What the hell you waiting for? A tip? Get out of here!" Peter said, trying to stifle the laughter as he watched him quickly drive away. The backlights of the car disappeared around the corner, and Peter tried to compose himself before he walked over to the couple still kneeling next to their bloodied suitcases.

CHAPTER **29**

"I HAVE APPLIED to several schools, including Darrow, and hope you get accepted somewhere." Mary said.

"Ill get in, don't worry," Peter said. "By the way Mum, I saw Captain Rob and he asked me to go sailing with him, and I said I would ask you."

"Captain Rob who owns the *Windstar*?"

"Yes. I want to go sailing with him."

"Captain Rob is a nice enough man but he has a hazy reputation."

"What do you mean?"

"They say that on land he is friendly, but on the ocean he is a pirate."

Peter liked the sound of it.

"He supposedly takes fruits and vegetables to the other islands, but some say that in fact he is a smuggler."

"What does he smuggle?"

"I can only guess. I just don't want you to get in trouble and you know it's rough out there on the ocean on a boat like that." The memory of her trip on the schooner to the island came flooding back.

"Yes, mum, I know that and I still want to go."

"How long would the trip last?"

"I don't know. A few weeks I guess. Please, Mum."

"Let me think about it," she said.

It had been a gusty day and Angus was at the tiller of

Barnacle. Peter sat next to him, thinking of his years at Saint Mary's that had come to an end. Now, gliding off the island's shoreline, he watched the pockets of warm rain move against the mountain landscape, forming ephemeral rainbows in its path. The lapping of the water against the hull and intermittent puffs of wind were the only sounds until Angus started singing.

"Fly me to the Moon," he belted out and Peter's looked at him and rolled his eyes.

"Angus, please, in case you didn't notice, it's already raining."

"Fill my heart with song, and let me sing forevermore," he kept singing.

"Where do you get those songs from?"

"That's Frankie! I sound just like him don't I?"

"Well, let's say it's a good thing no one else can hear you," Peter said. "Hey! Look! Isn't that the *Windstar?*" Peter pointed at a boat on the horizon.

"I think so. Why?"

"Because I'm going sailing on it."

"Are you serious?" Angus said.

"Yeah mon."

"You don't know about Cap'n Rob?"

"What about him?"

"He's a smuggler! A pirate! He'll take your white ass and trade it for a case of rum. Why do you think they call him Cap'n Rob?"

"Oh, you're funny. First of all, I would fetch more than a case of rum and anyway, I always wanted to be a pirate."

"Yeah, right, and your mother is letting you go with him?" Angus asked in disbelief.

"She hasn't said yes but I'm working on her. The Cap'n

leaves in a week for Barbados."

"I hope you realize that sailing on that boat isn't like sailing on this cruiser. It's pretty damn rough out there."

"I'll make it, and I am going if she will let me," Peter said.

"You're mad. And don't say I didn't warn you." Angus said as he looked out at the schooner sailing towards them.

The next day Mary got the call that Maria had died in her sleep. She went up to the estate and picked up her body and delivered it to the morgue. Arrangements were made for her burial, which had to be done quickly because of the heat. The Methodist minister conducted the ceremony in the middle of the day with only Mary, Viola, Christian and Peter in attendance. The funeral was quick and simple, and he felt deep sadness, knowing that he had lost a great teacher.

The Green Parrot was a small restaurant on the bay front that Mary had acquired with the last of her inheritance. She left the position at the bank for a business of her own and was happy for the change. It was another busy morning and the crowded restaurant suddenly seemed to darken as a giant of a man walked through the door. His face was black as coal and his penetrating eyes were barely visible under the cap pulled tightly over his huge head. He wore a loose cotton shirt torn at the shoulder and grease stains down the front, the thin fabric stretched tight against his massive shoulders. Mary had expected the captain to visit when she saw the *Windstar* drop anchor in front of the restaurant.

"Cap'n Rob, good to see you!" Mary held out her hand, which was quickly lost in his grip.

"Hello, ma'am. It's good to see you too. I understand your boy want to go sailing with me?" His voice was like a clap of thunder and all heads turned.

"That's what he tells me. What do you think?" Mary put her hands on her waist and stared at the captain.

"He's been after me for a while about dis and so if you say so, then it's okay with me,"

"Captain, that's great, but he is no rough crewman like what you have on your boat. He's never even been off the island before and quite honestly, I don't know where you go or what you use your boat for, and you probably noticed that he is a little different from everyone else, so I'm worried about his safety."

The captain's teeth flashed while he put his hands in his pockets and looked around at her customers who were now all silent, pretending not to be listening.

"You're right. My boat ain't no pleasure yacht and it ain't going to be no sweet cruise, but if he want to go to sea, I wouldn't hold him back. De boy ready to strike out and have some fun. I go take care of him, I promise you dat, and I bring him back alive."

Mary noticed he avoided the question about the use of the boat, but she liked his disarming manner, and what he said made sense. She needed to let him go. "I'm not crazy about the idea, but if you promise his safe return Cap'n, then he can go."

"No problem. Tell him to be on de jetty day after tomorrow. We leave in de afternoon." He turned and walked out of the restaurant, and with the passing of his shadow, the conversations quickly turned to whispers.

Two days later the dingy bumped into the landing platform below him, and Peter looked at the man at the oars. His brown face was rugged and scarred with an earring in one ear, and he looked up at Peter and his mouth dropped slightly, displaying two missing teeth.

"De Cap'n send me to get you. You de one coming on de boat?"

"Yeah, that's me!" Peter said. He grabbed his bag and stepped in and sat down in front of man, noticing the long scar on his forearm.

The oarsman never took his eyes off his passenger and kept shaking his head as he rowed towards the schooner. The captain was waiting on the deck with a group of men who stared curiously at the white boy. "Come aboard!" he roared.

Peter reached up and the captain grabbed his hand, picking him up into the air and depositing him onto a bag of copra in one quick motion. "Get ready, we leaving soon," he said and walked back to the stern of the boat.

Peter surveyed his surroundings, instantly aware of the sweet, pungent smell of the sun-dried coconuts in the bags piled high on the decks. He looked back at the captain who was leaning over some charts and found the gaze of daunting eyes upon him. A pang of fear engulfed him as he thought about what he had gotten himself into, and he stared back at the group of motley men, all very large and black except for the brown oarsman who rowed him out. They wore filthy tattered clothes with knives at their sides, and their bodies rippled with muscles dripping in sweat. Peter moved cautiously over the bags and stood timidly in front of the group.

"Where can I put this?" he asked, holding up his bag.

"Throw it down dere," a tall man cleaning a fish with a knife answered and pointed to an opening on the deck. "But you can't sleep dere" he added.

"Why not?" Peter asked.

The men exchanged amused glances." You know what? Try it out, maybe you'll like it," the fish man said. Peter walked over and peered down into the dark hole. "Let me ask you. You ever been to sea before?"

"Not really. Not too far from shore anyway," he answered.

"Den what de hell you doing here?"

Peter looked at him and the fear returned. "Don't worry, I'll be all right," he said.

"Yeah, just wait till tomorrow," another crewman said, and they all laughed.

The sound of the captain's booming voice coming from the stern made them all stop and turn. "Raise de anchor! Hoist de sail! Let's go!" He was standing next to the wheel, pointing at the horizon.

Peter watched as the crew jumped to their stations, and the heavy canvas sail glided slowly up the mast. The sound of the anchor chain being winched aboard sent vibrations throughout the boat and then a final crunch as the lines were tied off. There was a loud ruffling and a snap of the mainsail as it caught the wind, and the boat leaned over and started moving through the water away from the shore. Peter looked back towards the shrinking island and his fear was overtaken by a sinking sense of regret.

He began to understand the crew's concern about his own seaworthiness when the boat hit the southern end of the island and got the full force of the Atlantic. The reality became very apparent after an hour of feeling the swells of the ocean in the deep channel and his first surge of nausea. The aspiring pirate was soon clutching the side and emptied everything he could into the rolling sea below him.

The wind was blowing hard as the crimson sun settled on the horizon. Totally depleted, he climbed back over some bags of copra and groped his way down the ladder below where he had dropped his bag, only to find that the stench and heat overpowering. He lay down on the hard bunk and let out a weak scream when he felt his face crawling with cockroaches, feasting on the drying vomit. Moaning, he quickly crawled back up the steep companionway and flopped down on a bag of the foul smelling cargo. As the wind howled and the waves splashed over the gunwales, he tried to wedge himself next to the mast between a bag of copra and a large basket of vegetables that smelled of rotting turnips. He looked up at the dark sky now emblazoned with stars, and asked the good Lord to come to his rescue. The whipping wind was cold, but the rising heat from the bags kept him warm. There he spent his first night, listening to the howling of the wind and his own whimpers, mixed in with the creaking of the boom as it strained against the mast.

The next day the scorching sun shed its light on the pathetic boy who lay inert amongst the bags. Too weak to care, Peter stayed there for the whole day and into the next night, not moving except to reach for the occasional cups of tepid water offered by Aska, one of the crew. He drank what he could, poured the rest over his burning face, and handed the cup back, thanking him weakly. The ocean was too rough to move anywhere on deck so he urinated in his pants, the smell of which only added to the repugnance of his surroundings.

The merciless sun started early the next day and the stultifying heat fried his frail white body until the captain himself came over to see if there was any life left in him.

"Hey mon, you dead yet?" he asked, grinning.

Peter stared up at him, trying to decide.

"Here, drink dis, it will help, and keep your face out of de sun." The captain reached down and held him up by his back and moved a tin cup to his mouth. Peter wasn't sure of the concoction but it felt good going down. His hunger and thirst had taken second place to the nausea that continuously overwhelmed him. The captain lay him back down and threw him a damp and smelly rag to cover his face.

The day dragged on and Peter felt certain that his short and reckless life was quickly coming to an end. He began reciting all the prayers he had memorized at school, asking for a passing angel to swoop down and take him off the vessel from hell. He cursed himself for having ever left dry ground, and his moaning was drowned out by the howling wind and the thrashing of the boat against the rolling sea. The spray felt refreshing in the daytime but at night his wet clothes were clammy and damp and the chill was intensified by the incessant wind. On the dawn of fourth day, the sea grew calmer and with the little strength remaining, he sat up and felt the boat stabilize as they entered smoother water off an island in the distance.

"Barbados!" Aska said, standing over him and pointing to the horizon. He reached down and handed him a tin cup and a piece of bread. Peter dipped the bread in the tea and chewed slowly, realizing how weak he had become. He felt like death and smelled like a rat, savoring the sustenance he was given.

"Hey, you all right?" Aska's voice lacked any semblance of real sympathy. Peter nodded slowly and leaned against the mast, looking at the other three crewmen staring at him with mocked grimaces on their faces.

By dusk the vessel was moored in The Careenage, the deep-water harbor in the center of Bridgetown, the capital of Barbados. He felt life slowly creeping back as he sat on the deck drinking water and watching the passing cars, and listening to the singsong Bajan accent of passers-by, all of whom threw him curious glances.

He looked up to see Cap'n Rob standing over him. "You feeling better?" He handed him a piece of fried plantain, which Peter took and held in his hand. "Yes, Cap'n, I'm all right now, but I wasn't feeling so good before."

"I know dat, but you going to be okay, and when we go back out to sea, it's going to be easier."

"I hope so, because that was not fun." Peter's mouth twitched and he looked down at the food held between his filthy fingers. The captain nodded, picked up his bag and jumped over the side of the boat and on to the sidewalk. There was a car waiting for him with the door open. He got in and it moved quickly down the busy street.

The crew had spread some canvas over the boom, covering the stern and creating a shade from the scorching sun. It was humid and muggy sitting at the dock without a breeze, and by noon, everyone huddled under the shelter, drinking beer and watching the busy town pass by. Peter joined them, still feeble, and Aska moved over to give him a place to sit.

"So you make it. Dat's good," Aska said. By now Peter had learned the names of the other crewmen. There was Sanka, Belmont, and Anslem, and they all had become friendlier, almost accepting, of their white partner. A bottle of beer was passed to him, which he gingerly raised to his parched lips. It felt good going down and he nodded in appreciation.

"Thank you. It tastes good."

They laughed and raised their bottles to him, and he felt that he had just passed another test.

The group chatted and drank beer into the evening. Curious people walking by would stop and stare at him, and he realized that he was indeed an anomaly. Without a shirt or shoes, long matted hair and white skin, dark from the sun and dirt, and with a knife on his belt, he was a strange addition to the already portentous looking vessel. Some would stop and ask questions, and he realized he was the first white crewmember they had seen on these schooners, and when they heard he was from Dominica, he became even more of a curiosity. Although the crew was enjoying the attention, they said the Captain would not like it, and the comment puzzled Peter.

"Why not?" he asked Belmont.

"Because de Cap'n here on private business and he don't want any interference, dat's all."

"I see," said Peter.

"Don't worry about it. Just be cool, all right?" said Belmont, handing him another cold beer.

"No problem," he said, and they touched bottles and drank.

He spent the next two days eating and exploring Bridgetown and felt restored and invigorated.

"Where does the Cap'n stay when he's here?" He asked over another beer.

Aska looked at him and smiled. "Let's just say dat a woman has something to do with it."

"I see. And when are we going to leave?"

There was a silence. Anslem took a long drag on his cigarette. "Just relax, and stop asking too many questions," he said.

His uneasiness was assuaged two days later when a truck pulled up in the early morning to unload their cargo of copra, a process that took most of the day. The bags were taken from the hold in the boat to a line of the crew that passed them up to the deck and on to the truck. It was backbreaking work in the blazing sun and yet Peter was able to keep up with the rest of the crew that were seemingly impressed. By sunset, the boat had been unloaded and cleaned, and now they all sat exhausted on the deck under the canvas, smoking and drinking local beer. They drank and joked into the evening and Sanka produced a meal of fresh fish and yams, which was quickly devoured.

"So what cargo do we take back?" Peter asked. There was a silence and they all looked at him. Another question he shouldn't have asked, he thought.

"You will find out soon enough." Belmont said, and he just nodded, remembering the smuggling comments his mother had made.

"No problem," he said, feeling all eyes on him.

"And make sure you don't ask de captain dat question, okay?" Aska said.

"No problem," he said, grinning to himself.

For the next three days the boat bounced gently against the dock while everyone waited and Peter explored the quaint town. There was a statue of Lord Nelson in the center where the traffic all converged. He sat next to it, watching the people go by, fascinated by the number of white faces he saw. Although he had cleaned most of the dirt off his body, he was still dressed in ragged shorts and shirt with no shoes, and many stopped and stared at him, some with pity on their faces.

He had enough money to go to a movie. After *Jailhouse Rock* he came out snapping his fingers, thinking how he could comb his hair like Elvis. He bought a jar of Brylcream and found that it kept the hair out of his eyes, piled on top in what the crew called a "Beebop", and he felt pretty cool. He now stood on the deck under the canvas cover doing his Elvis moves and talking in a Bajan accent, much to the amusement of the crew and pedestrians. Nevertheless, the Elvis look didn't last long when he discovered that the grease made a mess of everything he touched and the combing operation took too much time, and he was soon looking like himself again.

Windstar in Barbados

Peter with "Bebop"

CHAPTER **30**

THE CAPTAIN APPEARED suddenly five days later and announced that the boat would be leaving that evening and wanted food and water taken aboard immediately. Peter was about to ask about cargo but remembered the warning. They prepared the boat and waited for nightfall when they slipped away from the dock and out of the harbor. It was a moonless night and no running lights were on as they moved up the island's coast until they reached a strip of land that sat in darkness. The anchor splashed into the water and Peter looked towards the shore and listened to the crashing of waves while they all sat silently. He was about to ask the purpose of the exercise when he saw flashes of light coming from the shore and the captain quickly responded with three short bursts from his flashlight. He heard the sound of an approaching engine and watched a large freighter pulled up alongside. Everyone moved quickly and boxes were passed up on deck and stored below. An hour later, as the last box went down, a large man in a cap exchanged small packages with the captain, and the freighter pulled away. The sails were raised and the *Windstar* headed out to the open sea.

The crew settled down for the trip and Peter looked closely at one of the boxes and read *Mount Gay Rum -- Product of Barbados*. Rum, he thought; it made sense so far, and he smiled to himself as the boat headed south for the French island of Martinique. They were "running with the wind" and by now, he had acquired his "sea legs" and without the smell of the copra, the journey was a pleasant one. The laden boat glided over the top of large swells and down into the trough of the next one, and the budding pirate felt content.

The captain followed a similar routine off the lee side of Martinique, anchoring off a dark side of the island. Some light signals came from shore and a large barge pulled up alongside. Muffled words were exchanged in French patois and the crew quickly unloaded the rum from below. With only a flicker of light in the hatch, they worked quickly and as soon as the barge pulled away, another one pulled up alongside, laden with a different cargo. Peter's curiosity was soon satisfied as he saw the labels of French wine and champagne go past him and stored below. The sun was peeking over the distant mountaintop when the last case was stored and the exhausted crew pulled up anchor, raised the sails, and headed south.

It was two more days of pleasant sailing on calmer seas before the loaded schooner dropped its sails a mile off the small island of St. Barts. In the same fashion there was an exchange of flashing lights and the French liquor was exchanged for cases of Gordon's gin and English whiskey. The sails went up at dawn, and the boat was once again under way.

In a private moment with Aska, Peter asked about the operation. He explained how the boat started with a cargo of copra and vegetables, which was checked by customs in Barbados, and then liquor was taken from islands that paid no duty to islands with a heavy import duty tax on foreign booze. The French imposed an onerous tax on the Barbados rum, but not on the wine and champagne from France. St. Barts had a levy on the French liquor but not on the gin and whiskey that was going to Dominica. Because of the amount of liquor exchanged, the tax savings meant several thousand dollars to the smugglers and a handsome profit for the captain.

Under a cloudless sky, the *Windstar* sailed across the channel separating the islands until the wind died suddenly and they were caught in the doldrums. Without a breath of air and low on petrol, there was little choice but to sit in the middle of the channel, slowly rocking back and forth in the calm turquoise water. The day had a magical ending as the sunset produced an "Emerald Drop" -- the two seconds when a green flash emanated and the sun sank behind the cloudless horizon.

Their journey was almost over, so some of the good rum was passed around. Peter sat on the deck, looking darker and wilder, and sang and cursed with the rest of the rogues, and he felt very content. He looked back at the captain standing like a giant shadow watching him, and saw the flash of a wide smile.

The schooner approached the rugged silhouette of Dominica and he felt sad, knowing that his adventure would soon be over. It had been five weeks since they had left its shores and when the captain ordered the sails dropped, he knew it was to stall and wait for nightfall and avoid detection while he disposed of the last of his illegal cargo. Peter recognized the cove from where the flashing lights came, and he understood the language of the men who came out to the boat to unload it. There was surprise and concern when they saw him on board, but the captain assured them that he was, "No problem."

The smugglers left with the liquor and now the full moon reflected off the water, illuminating the island in a

warm glow. The sweet scent of the frangipani flowers drifted across the water and Peter gazed at his island as a flying fish broke the glassy surface in front of him. He took
a gulp of French wine and stared at the moon, and as if
in a trance, stood up and walked to the bow, where he
stripped himself naked and stared down at the golden garden before him. He dove in, breaking the surface in silent
ripples and felt the warmth envelop him. He swam several
yards and treaded water, looking back at the boat rocking
slowly in the moonlight. It appeared as if in a dream, unat-
tached, and floating before him with the dim light from the
lantern at the end of the boom, twinkling in the distance.
He swam slowly back and could hear the laughter of the
crew huddled around the stern. He climbed aboard, dried
off, pulled his clothes back on and became acutely aware
of their smell and the stench he had been living with. He
pushed his hair out of his eyes and went to join the crew
that greeted him with pats on the back.

"Hey, Peter! Come here. I have something for you."
Captain Rob was sitting on the wheelhouse, the silhouette of
a giant.

Peter watched as he picked up a cup and poured him
some champagne.

"Thanks, Cap'n. I never drank champagne before."

The captain laughed and raised his cup. "And I bet it's not
the only thing you have never done before dis trip."

"You right, Cap'n, and I thank you for that."

There was laughter behind him and he turned to look at
the faces of his friends that saluted him with their cups. He sat
for a long time drinking champagne, laughing and joking with
the greatest group of scoundrels he had ever known.

"I never think de white boy make de trip after the first few days, and then when he start putting down de rum and laughing about de cargo dat come on de boat, I think dat this boy all right." Aska raised his cup.

"He make a good smuggler," Belmont said. "In fact, I think he must come from an old family of pirates." Everyone laughed and more champagne was passed around.

"I hear you're leaving the island soon?" Aska said.

"I'm going to America."

"How you can leave Paradise and go dere? I hear America is a crazy place."

"I want to see for myself. This is all I know, and if I have nothing to compare it to, how do I know this is paradise?"

"You have a point. My guess is you will find out quick enough and come back." Aska poured more champagne into everyone's cups.

They talked and laughed into the night and the stories of the trip became exaggerated, but no one seemed to care. Peter's head was spinning and he got up and walked unsteadily to the foredeck. He found the same spot next to the mast where he had spent his first horrific nights, and in a bed of dried banana leaves, he stared up at the sky, and as the moon looked down on him from its own bed of stars, he wished for no tomorrow.

The next day no one stirred until the scorching sun and barking captain forced pounding heads from where they lay. The anchor was hoisted and sails were raised as the *Windstar* coasted gently off the familiar shore until the sight of red roofs and the Roseau bay front came into view. He listened to the final splash of the anchor and the sounds of the busy town drifting out to the boat. He stuffed the remains of his filthy clothes into his bag and threw it into the rowboat next to Aska. He said his farewells to his friends and turned to thank the captain.

"You did good," Captain Rob said. "And don't forget, what happened on de boat, stay on de boat, all right?"

"No problem Cap'n," Peter replied.

The captain handed him some folded bills. Peter took them and looked up at the captain. "You don't have to pay me Cap'n, I wasn't expecting it."

"No, man, you did all right. Take it."

"Thanks Cap'n." They shook hands and Peter felt the giant vice of his grip for the last time.

Aska rowed him back to the jetty, and he looked back at the schooner rocking gently in the dark blue water, and waved at the rest of the pirates that were now all hanging on to the rigging. He said his farewell to Aska, and walked down the street towards the Green Parrot. He felt the bills in his pocket and realized it was the first money he had ever earned, and it was as a smuggler. He giggled and walked into the restaurant.

Familiar faces from the tables looked up at him in alarm as he approached the counter where his mother was pouring a beer. Her mouth fell open and the beer spilled onto the table. The room got quiet and Peter looked around, reading the astonishment. His skin was a tanned and dirty brown, his matted hair hung down to his eyes, his tattered shirt was filthy, and his short pants were held up by a piece of rope with his knife still synched to his waist. The slight breeze that came through the doors spread the pungent odor that permeated his body.

"Hi Mum. I'm back," he said standing before her.

Her hands came out before her. "Dear Mother of God! You're alive!" she shouted.

"Why wouldn't I be?"

"Jesus Christ, child! You left over a month ago on an ominous looking boat. You were supposed to be back two weeks ago and I have had no word from you! My God! I am thrilled you are back!"

They hugged and she quickly moved back a step. "Christ, look at you! And what in God's name is that smell?" Everyone in the restaurant laughed.

On the way home Mary pulled off the road overlooking the ocean. "I have some bad news for you," she said.

"What?" he asked and the dream of going to America exploded in his mind.

"It's Christian," she said. "He was found dead in his garden. A tree fell on him and killed him."

"Oh, no!" There was a silence. "When is the funeral?"

"There is none. He had to be buried quickly. I guess he had been there for a few days before he was found. I'm so sorry. I know what he meant to you." Mary waited as he quickly got out of the car and walked away, unable to stop the heaving of his chest.

The days that followed were full of questions about his sailing trip, and Mary ceased probing when she realized she was not going to get any details. The obvious truth was revealed three weeks later when the *Windstar* was returning from Guadeloupe and severe weather forced the vessel onto a reef, and it sank with the top of the mast left sticking out of the water. The captain and crew swam ashore but the boat was full of contraband wine, whiskey, and rum and had settled neatly on the shallow reefs. By sunrise the word had spread and it didn't take long for the villagers to swim out to salvage the precious cargo. For days after, the entire village fell into a drunken stupor with everyone singing, laughing, or staggering down the middle of the street.

Peter was sad at the loss of the boat but viewed the village spectacle as hilarious, and Mary became quickly aware of what his trip on the "trading schooner" had entailed. Upset at her own naiveté but pleased that he was not there when the boat sank, she managed to find some humor in it all but little satisfaction in her son now being referred to as "Peter the Pirate."

CHAPTER **31**

THE REJECTIONS FROM schools brought a mood of despondency until the acceptance came from Darrow, where he would be joining Ivan. When Mary announced that an old friend from Vassar would be visiting the island with her son from upstate New York, Peter was excited to find out what was in store for him from someone who would know. Mary brought them to the house and Peter was introduced to Ben, a tall, well-built young man with a crew-cut.

There was little dialog during the day of sightseeing while the visitors observed some of the island in silent bewilderment. Back at the house they watched the sun sink on the horizon, and Peter and Ben walked onto the lawn and sat on the grass overlooking the dense valley below.

"This is one beautiful island you live on," Ben said. "How long have you been here?"

"All my life," Peter said.

"You were born here?

"Yes, I was."

"Have you ever been off the island?"

"Only once. I sailed to a couple of the other islands. It was pretty cool."

"I bet. "But you've never been to the States, right?"

"Never, and I can hardly wait."

Ben looked at him and said, "My friend, you are in for a big surprise."

"Why is that?"

"From what I have seen of your island, this place is a world of its own."

"What do you mean?"

"Everything here seems so safe and no one seems to have any worries. I understand that you are one of the few white people on the island and yet that doesn't seem to be a problem for you?"

"Why would that be a problem? I'm sometimes called a 'beke blanc' but that just means white boy. It's never been a problem."

Ben stared at him, and slowly shook his head. "In the States, there is a lot of discrimination. Black people don't have the same freedoms as whites, and in some parts of the country, there is incredible prejudice. Now the blacks are trying to claim their freedom and there are riots. It's not pretty."

"Are you serious? How long has this been going on?"

"Since the birth of the country, since slavery."

"Jesus Christ. I didn't know that."

"In fact," said Ben, "it's not just blacks, there's prejudice against Jews, homosexuals, anything that is not accepted by the white majority. Shit man, there is even some prejudice against women."

Peter squinted his eyes at Ben. "What's a Jew? What's a homosexual?"

"You're kidding me. I can't believe you're asking me these questions. You don't know?" He looked closely at Peter, then looked away and continued talking. "A Jew is someone who believes in Judaism as the only true religion. In the States there is prejudice against them because they are different and have a religion with a history of persecution. Remember Hitler? He tried to eradicate every Jew in Germany."

Peter nodded his head. "I read about that. So what's a homosexual?"

Ben looked away again and was silent for a minute. "You really don't know?" he asked.

"No, I don't. Should I?"

"It's when two people of the same sex are together as a couple." He looked sideways at Peter for a reaction.

Peter looked at him, not sure what to say. "You mean like my mom and Hazel?"

"Exactly," Ben said.

"And homosexuals are not accepted in the States?"

"Well, let's say they are just not understood and for the most part, not accepted, at least not yet."

"This discrimination thing isn't something I'm looking forward to."

Ben looked at him. "Prejudice is a fact of life, my friend."

"It hasn't been for me. And I've never thought of my mother as anything but my mother, and I've never heard her called a homosexual before. They sleep together, but I never realized that was wrong."

"It's not wrong. It's just not seen as normal." Ben looked down at his hands, as if to regret the conversation.

The two looked at each other "So tell me," Ben said. "Why would you ever want to leave this place?"

It took a few moments for Peter to absorb all that had been said. "Not sure I do now, but I want to see what's out there, on the other side of the fence."

"That's cool. I understand," Ben replied. "You will like the States, but you will appreciate this island for what it is."

Their conversation was interrupted by three long blasts of the ship's horn coming from the harbor. Beth was shouting from the upstairs veranda "We have to leave! Now!"

Peter walked to the house and said his goodbyes while Mary hustled them into the car and back to the boat. He thought about his conversation with Ben and his excitement about leaving the island was now tempered with the notion of entering a world of alien realities. He wondered if his mother had done him wrong by not telling him about what her relationship with Hazel meant, and that black people, the only friends he ever had, were treated badly in America.

Departure day drew near and he started noticing things he had always taken for granted. He relished the laughter, the grandeur of the landscape, the richness of the land, and the sounds and fragrances as he drove through the villages.

A group of friends surrounded him when he came out from the airline office.

"Hey mon, don't be gone long. We waiting for you, okay?"

"No problem. I'll be back." They chatted, laughed, and slapped him on the back before he turned and made his way up the street towards Saint Mary's.

The grounds were empty and he saw the Brothers walking slowly back and forth next to the school, with heads bowed and rosaries between the palms of their hands, He waited under the tree where he had stood so many times before. He closed his eyes, listening to the murmur of the distant prayers mixed in with the sound of birds above him, and became absorbed in memories.

He opened his eyes to see the outline of Brother Gorman before him.

"Praying?" the Brother asked.

"Yes Brother, and giving thanks." Their eyes locked and the Brother put out his hand and Peter took it. "I came to say good-bye, Brother, and to thank you for everything."

"I was doing God's work. I must admit, He made it a bit

of a challenge at times, but it made me a better servant." He paused before he spoke again, "Please don't become a stranger to us. Remember, these are your roots."

"Don't worry, Brother. I won't."

"And it's never too late to become a Catholic. You would be a good one." Brother Gorman said with a grin.

"Thanks, Brother, I'll remember that." They shook hands again and he walked back towards the iron gates. He turned and saw the Brothers standing together and waving. He waved back and blinked twice to clear his watering eyes.

The day was overcast when he said farewell to Hazel, Evelyn and Ray. He heard the dogs barking and the parrot screeching as he walked down the stone steps to the car. Mary said very little as they drove down the steep hill, through the villages and past familiar faces on the long road to the other side of the island. They passed the spot where Seamon had the episode with the Manicou, and Peter chuckled to himself. Minutes later Mary pulled off the road under a large tree.

"Why are we stopping?" Peter asked as she turned off the engine. She said nothing and he looked out the window and heard a soft cooing, and stared at the two doves standing on the branch above him. He looked back at her.

"Peter, there is something I want to tell you before you leave." He looked at her and waited for her to continue. "It's about Hazel and me." She spoke slowly.

Peter held up his hand. "It's okay, Mum. I know already."

"You do? You never said anything." There was a momentary silence. "I don't want you to think I was hiding anything from you. You may as well know that she is the reason I stayed here and didn't go back to the States, and it was a hard decision because I wanted to do what was best for the three of you."

"I'm glad you stayed. This is my home." He looked out at the dense foliage all around him.

There was more silence except for the cooing coming from above. He turned and touched her hand. "Thank you for telling me," He said.

She remained silent and started the car. They moved down the steep hill and through two more villages before she parked in front of the small airport terminal.

Peter got out quickly, grabbed his suitcase and walked through the door, looking for Rosemarie. He spotted her at the counter and walked over. She looked up and dropped her pen.

"It's you again! My island boy! You come to see me?" she said with a dimpled smile.

"Yes, it's me," Peter said, remembering how beautiful she was. He handed her his ticket.

She looked at his ticket and up at him. "You didn't come to see me, you leaving me!" She stamped his ticket. "All this time I've been waiting for you and when you finally come, you ready to leave." She laughed.

"You like to tease me, don't you? But, yes, I'm leaving," Peter said. He caught the smell of her perfume and the memories came rushing back.

She took his suitcase and looked at him. "So now I have to keep waiting for you. That's okay. I will wait. But make sure you come back, okay?"

"Well, it might not be right away, but I'll be back, and next time, don't run away from me, okay?" he said, smiling.

She passed him his ticket and gave his hand a quick squeeze. "Okay, island boy, I'll be here for you." Peter's gaze lingered before he moved away, letting the woman behind him take his place.

Peter and his mother stood together waiting, and there was an uncomfortable silence between them while he kept sending furtive glances to Rosemarie. Mary was giving him last minute instructions but soon the roar of the approaching plane drowned out her words, and they walked to the door. A pretty girl motioned for Peter and four other passengers to board. He turned and looked at his mother who opened her arms wide and he rushed into them.

She clutched him tightly and put his face between her hands and kissed his forehead.

"I will miss you terribly. Take care of yourself, and please write."

"I love you, Mum."

He picked up his bag and walked towards the plane and climbed up the small ladder. He turned and waved, ducked his head, and quickly found a seat. The small plane went to the end of the short runway and turned. His neck snapped back as it raced towards the ocean. He felt it lift off, and looked out the window and saw his mother standing outside with Rosemarie next to her, waving to her island boy. His face bumped into the glass as he tried not to lose sight of them, but the thrill of the ride quickly overtook the emotion of leaving his treasured world behind, and he leaned back and closed his eyes, and felt the throbbing of his anticipating heart.

ACKNOWLEDGMENTS

I want to acknowledge the following people: Leslie Keenan, my writing coach who helped me on this journey, Alexander Collins for the cover design, and my family, for encouraging me to start and finish the story.

CPSIA information can be obtained
at www.ICGtesting.com
Printed in the USA
FSHW010616200719
60211FS

9 781478 726616